The Seagull Sartre Library

The Seagull Sartre Library

The Seagull Sartre Library

VOLUME 11

ON NOVELS
AND NOVELISTS

JEAN-PAUL SARTRE

TRANSLATED BY
CHRIS TURNER

LONDON NEW YORK CALCUTTA

INDIA

This work is published with the support of
Institut français en Inde – Embassy of France in India

✳

Seagull Books, 2021

ISBN 978 0 8574 2 914 8

British Library Cataloguing-in-Publication Data
A catalogue record for this book is available
from the British Library

Typeset by Seagull Books, Calcutta, India
Printed and bound in the USA by Integrated Books International

CONTENTS

*

MONSIEUR FRANÇOIS MAURIAC
AND FREEDOM

The novel doesn't present things, but their signs.[1] How, with these mere signs—words—which are *indications* in a void, can we make a world that holds up? How is it that Stavrogin is alive? We would be wrong to believe he draws his life from my imagination: words give rise to images when we muse on them, but when I read, I am not musing: I am deciphering. No, I do not imagine Stavrogin. I await him, I await his acts and the end of his adventure. This dense matter I stir around when I read Dostoevsky's *Demons* is my own expectancy, my time.[2] For a book is either merely a little pile of dry leaves

---

1 I could equally well have penned the following remarks about more recent works, such as *Mamôna* [eventually published as *Les chemins de la mer* (Trans.)] or *Plongées*. But when he wrote *The End of the Night*, Monsieur Mauriac's stated aim was to deal with the problem of freedom. This is why I have preferred to take my examples from this book.

2 Fyodor Dostoevsky, *Demons* (Richard Pevear and Larissa Volkhonsky trans.) (London: Vintage, 1994). Also known in English as *The*

or, alternatively, a great form in movement: the act of reading. The novelist seizes upon this movement, guides and inflects it; he makes it the substance of his characters. A novel, a succession of acts of reading, of little parasitic lives, each of them no more than the length of a dance, swells with, and feeds on, its readers' time. But, for my periods of impatience and ignorance to be caught, shaped and, ultimately, presented to me as the flesh of these invented creatures, the novelist has to know how to draw them into his trap. He has to hollow out in his book, by means of the signs available to him, a time similar to mine, in which the future is not decided. If I suspect the future actions of the hero are determined in advance by heredity, social influences or some other mechanism, my own time ebbs back to me and I am left there alone, reading and persisting in the face of a motionless book. Do you want your characters to live? Make them free. The thing is not to define, nor even less to explain, unforeseeable acts and passions (in a novel, the best psychological analyses reek of death), but merely to *present* them. What Rogogine is going to do, neither he nor I know. I know he is going to see his guilty mistress again, and yet I cannot guess whether he will control himself or whether excess of anger will drive him to murder: he is free. I slip into him and there he is, awaiting his own self with my expectancy. *Inside me*, he is afraid of himself; he is alive.

Possessed. Though Camus adapted the work for the French stage as *Les Possédés*, Sartre uses the more accurate title, *Les Démons*. [Trans.]

As I was about to begin reading *The End of the Night*,[3] it occurred to me that Christian authors are, by the nature of their belief, the best placed to write novels. The man of religion is free. The supreme forebearance of Catholics may irritate us, because it is something learned, but if they are novelists, it plays in their favour. Figures in a novel and Christians, being centres of indeterminacy, both have characters, but they have them in order to escape them. They are free above and beyond their natures and, if they give in to those natures, they do so once more out of freedom. They may get caught up in psychical mechanisms, but they will never be mechanical. Even the Christian notion of sin is strictly in keeping with the principles of the genre. The Christian sins and the hero of the novel also must transgress. The novel's duration, dense as it is, would lack the urgency that confers necessity and cruelty on the work of art, if the existence of the transgression—which cannot be wiped away and must be redeemed—didn't reveal to the reader the irreversibility of time. Dostoevsky too was a Christian novelist. Not a novelist *and* a Christian, in the way that Pasteur was a Christian *and* a scientist, but a novelist in the service of Christ.

---

3 François Mauriac, *La Fin de la nuit* (Paris: Grasset, 1935). The novel is the last of a series of four works that relate the history of Mauriac's character, Thérèse Desqueyroux. All four are published together, in an English translation by Gerard Hopkins, as *Thérèse* (Harmondsworth: Penguin, 1959). [Trans.]

Monsieur Mauriac is a Christian novelist too. And his book *La Fin de la Nuit* aims to plumb the depths of a woman's freedom. He tells us in his preface that what he is trying to depict is 'that power, granted to all human beings—no matter how much they may seem to be the slaves of a hostile fate—of saying "No" to the law which beats them down'.[4] We are at the heart of the art of the novel here, at the heart of faith. However, when I finish reading, I confess to feeling disappointed. Not for a moment was I sucked in; not for a moment did I forget *my* time. I existed and could feel myself living. I yawned a little, and at times said, 'Well played!' I thought more of François Mauriac than of Thérèse Desqueyroux.[5] Of Mauriac, refined, sensitive and narrow, with his unabashed discretion, his intermittent goodwill, his pathos that is a product of his nerves, his sour, stumbling poetry, his awkward style and sudden vulgarity. Why was I not able to forget him or myself? And what had become of this Christian predisposition towards novel-writing? We have to come back, here, to freedom. By what procedures does M. Mauriac reveal to us that freedom he has bestowed upon his heroine?

Thérèse Desqueyroux struggles against her destiny. So far, so good. She is, then, a twofold creature. One part of her is wholly encompassed by Nature; we can say of

---

4 François Mauriac, 'The End of the Night' in *La Fin de la nuit*, p. 161.

5 The central female character of the novel. [Trans.]

her that she is like this or like that, as we can of a pebble or a log. A whole other part escapes description and definition, because it is merely an absence. When freedom accepts Nature, then fate alone rules. When it rejects it and battles back against the grain, then Thérèse Desqueyroux *is free*. She has the freedom to say 'no'—or, at the very least, not to say 'yes' ('All that is asked of them is that they should not resign themselves to night's darkness').[6] A Cartesian, infinite, formless, nameless, fateless freedom, 'forever re-begun', whose only power is to assent, but which is sovereign because it can withhold that assent. This at least is how we glimpse that freedom in the preface. But will we find it in the novel?

We must say, to begin with, that this suspensive will seems more tragic than novelistic. Thérèse's vacillations between following the impulses of her nature and recovering her will are reminiscent of Rotrou's stanzas;[7] the true novelistic conflict is, rather, the battle freedom fights with itself. In Dostoevsky, freedom is poisoned at its very sources; it gets entangled at the very point where it seeks to unfurl itself. The pride and irascibility of Dmitri Karamazov are as free as Aliosha's profound peace. The nature that stifles him and with which he wrestles is not how God made him, but how he has made himself. It is what he has sworn to be, which has become fixed and

6 Mauriac, *Thérèse*, p. 161.

7 Jean de Rotrou (1609–50): a French poet and playwright, now remembered as one of the lesser lights of French theatre's golden age. [Trans.]

frozen by the irreversibility of time. Thinking along these same lines, Alain[8] says that a character is a solemn oath. Reading M. Mauriac—and perhaps this is to his credit—we muse on the possibility of another Thérèse, who would have been a more capable, greater character. But, ultimately, what commends this battle of freedom against nature to us is its venerable antiquity and orthodoxy. It is reason battling against the passions; it is the Christian soul, united to the body through the imagination, rebelling against the appetites of the body. Let us accept this theme provisionally, even if it doesn't seem true: its beauty might be thought a sufficient justification.

However, is this 'fatality' against which Thérèse must struggle really, solely, the determinism of her natural tendencies? M. Mauriac calls it destiny. But let us not confuse destiny and character. Character is still us; it is the set of mild forces that insinuates itself into our intentions, imperceptibly deflecting our efforts from them—always in the same direction. When Thérèse is angry with Mondoux, who has humiliated her, M. Mauriac writes: 'This time it really was she who was speaking, that Thérèse who was quite prepared to bite.'[9] This clearly concerns Thérèse's character. But a little later,

---

8 Alain was the pen name of the influential French philosopher Emile-Auguste Chartier (1868– 1951). As a teacher at the Lycée Henri IV, Alain counted Simone Weil, Georges Canguilhem and Raymond Aron among his pupils. [Trans.]

9 Mauriac, *La Fin de la Nuit*, p. 179. This passage is omitted from the edition from which the English translation was made. [Trans.]

as she is leaving, having managed to find a wounding riposte,[10] we read: 'The blow which she had delivered with so sure a hand had helped her to measure the extent of her power and take cognizance of her mission.'[11] What mission? Then I recall these words from the preface: 'the power she exercises to poison and corrupt'.[12] And here we have Destiny, encompassing and exceeding character, and representing within Nature, and in the— at times so basely psychological—*oeuvre* of M. Mauriac, the power of the Supernatural. As soon as Thérèse's acts escape her grasp, they are governed by a certain law, independent of Thérèse's will, a law that brings doom-laden consequences down on all of them, even the most well-intentioned. This reminds us of the punishment meted out by the fairy in the tale: 'Every time you open your mouth, toads will jump out.'[13] If you don't believe, then this sorcery will mean nothing to you. But the believer understands it very well: what is it, ultimately, but the expression of that other sorcery, original sin? I accept, then, that M. Mauriac is in earnest when he speaks, as a Christian, of Destiny. But when he speaks of it as a novelist, I can no longer follow him. Thérèse

---

10 I know of few scenes more vulgar than this one and the curious thing is that we clearly have to ascribe this vulgarity to M. Mauriac himself.

11 Mauriac, *Thérèse*, p. 275.

12 Mauriac, *Thérèse*, p. 161.

13 This is clearly a reference to Charles Perrault's tale, 'Les Fées' in *Perrault's Popular Tales* (Oxford: Clarendon Press, 1888).

Desqueyroux's destiny is the product, in part, of a flaw in her character and, in part, of a curse afflicting her actions. These two factors are not compatible: the one may be discerned from within by the heroine herself, the other would require an infinite series of observations made from outside by a witness bent on following all of Thérèse's undertakings through to their final consequences. So well does M. Mauriac knows this himself that, when he wants to have us see Thérèse as predestined, he resorts to artifice: he shows her to us as she appears *to others*: 'It was not surprising that people turned to look as she passed. An animal can be detected by its smell even before it is seen.'[14] This, then, is the great hybrid phenomenon revealed to us throughout the novel: Thérèse—but not limited to her pure freedom—as she eludes her own grasp and moves, in a baleful fog, towards her earthly destruction. But, in the end, how could Thérèse know she had a destiny, except by already having consented to it? And how does M. Mauriac know it? The idea of destiny is poetic and contemplative. But the novel is action and the novelist has no right to leave the field and ensconce himself comfortably on some hillock to assess the battle and muse on the Fortunes of War.

We shouldn't think M. Mauriac succumbed just the once, by chance, to the temptations of poetry: this way of first identifying with his character, then suddenly abandoning her and contemplating her from the outside,

---

14 Mauriac, *Thérèse*, p. 275.

like a judge, is characteristic of his art. He led us to believe, from the very first page, that he was going to tell the story by adopting Thérèse's standpoint; and, indeed, between our eyes and Thérèse's room, her servant and the rumours rising from the street, we immediately sense the translucent density of another consciousness. But a few pages further on, when we believe we are still inside that consciousness, we have already left it; we are outside, with M. Mauriac, taking a hard look at Thérèse. The fact is that, in order to pull off this illusion, M. Mauriac uses the novelistic ambiguity of the 'third person'. In a novel, the pronoun 'she' may refer to another person, that is to say, an opaque object, someone whom we only ever see from the outside. As, for example, when I write, 'I noticed *she* was trembling.' But it also happens that this pronoun takes us into an intimacy that should logically be expressed in the first person: 'She was astounded to hear her own words resonating.' This is something I can actually only know if *I* am *she* or, in other words, if I am able to write, 'I could hear my own words resonating.' Novelists actually use this entirely conventional mode of expression out of a sort of discretion, so as not to ask an unreserved complicity of the reader and to cover the dizzying intimacy of the 'I' with a kind of glaze. The heroine's consciousness represents the lens through which the reader can cast an eye on the world of the novel, and the word 'she' gives the illusion of a lens situated at some distance from the action; it reminds us that this revealing consciousness is also a novelistic creation, representing

with crime—at least not consciously.'[15] This leaves me in a strange situation: I *am* Thérèse, and she is myself with a degree of aesthetic distance. Her thoughts are my thoughts, and I form them as she does. And yet I have revelations about her that she doesn't have. Or, alternatively, I am located within the heart of her consciousness and help her to lie to herself, while, at the same time, I judge her, condemn her and put myself inside her as *another person*: 'She couldn't *not* have realized the lie she was acting: but now she nestled into it, seeking rest.'[16] This sentence is ample evidence of the constant betrayal M. Mauriac demands of me. Lying to herself, uncovering her lie and yet attempting to conceal it from herself —this is Thérèse's attitude, an attitude I can only know from her alone. But in the very way this attitude is revealed to me, there is a witness' merciless judgement. Moreover, this uneasy position doesn't last for long: under cover of that 'third person', the ambiguity of which I have noted, M. Mauriac suddenly slips outside his character, dragging me along with him: ' "How well that make-up suits you, dear . . ." Those were the first words that Thérèse spoke—the words of one woman to another.'[17] The lights of Thérèse's consciousness have gone out; no longer illuminated from within, she has reassumed her compact opacity. But neither the noun

---

15 Mauriac, *Thérèse*, p. 190.

16 Mauriac, *Thérèse*, p. 229.

17 Mauriac, *Thérèse*, p. 172.

nor the pronoun that refer to her have changed. Nor has the cast of the narrative. M. Mauriac even finds this to-ing and fro-ing so natural that he shifts from Thérèse-as-subject to Thérèse-as-object in the course of a single sentence: 'She heard nine o'clock strike. She must still find some way of killing time, for it was too early as yet to swallow the cachet which would assure her a few hours of sleep; *not that such was the habit of this cautious and desperate woman*, but tonight she could not resist its promise of help.'[18] Who is adjudging Thérèse a 'cautious and desperate woman' in this way? It cannot be she. No, it is M. Mauriac. It is myself. We have the Desqueyroux file before us and we are pronouncing judgement.

M. Mauriac's games don't end there: he likes to take hold of roofs by a corner and lift them, like Asmodeus, that prying, harum-scarum devil he is so fond of. When he finds it more convenient, he leaves Thérèse and suddenly goes and instals himself inside another mind—that of Georges, Marie, Bernard Desqueyroux or Anne the servant. He has a little look around, then disappears again the way puppets do.

Thérèse could read nothing on the averted face. She did not know that her daughter was thinking: 'In the whole of my life, I shall never

---

18 Mauriac, *Thérèse*, p. 169 (translation modified; the English translation is based on a different edition from that to which Sartre refers [Trans.]).

go half as far as this old woman has gone in the last few days.'[19]

She didn't know? Well, never mind. M. Mauriac suddenly abandons her, leaves her to her ignorance, jumps to Marie and brings back this little snapshot for us. By contrast, on other occasions he generously has one of his creatures share in the novelist's divine lucidity: 'She stretched out her arms, tried to draw him to her, but he broke violently from her touch. It was then she realized that she had lost him.'[20] Signs are uncertain and are binding only on the present, but what matter? M. Mauriac has decided that Georges is lost to Thérèse. He decided it the way the ancient Gods decreed Oedipus' parricide and incest. Then, to impart his decree to us, for a few moments he lends his creature the divinatory powers of Tiresias: have no fear, she will soon relapse into her darkness. And here, indeed, comes the curfew, at which point all consciousnesses are extinguished: a wearying M. Mauriac suddenly withdraws from all his characters at once and all that remains is the world's exterior, a few puppets in a cardboard landscape:

> The girl dropped her hand from before her eyes.
>
> 'I thought you were asleep.'
>
> Once more a note of supplication came into the elder woman's voice:

---

19 Mauriac, *Thérèse*, p. 311.

20 Mauriac, *Thérèse*, p. 256.

'Swear to me that you are happy.'[21]

Gestures and sounds in the shadows. A few feet away, M. Mauriac is sitting, musing:

> 'What terrible pain you must have been through, Mamma!'
>
> 'No, I felt nothing, except the prick when you used the hypodermic . . .'
>
> But that rattling in the throat and that congested face. Is it possible that human beings can go through such a hell of agony, yet keep no memory of it?

To anyone who knows the character of Marie, there can be no doubt that the young girl wastes no time on such thoughts. No, this is the creator resting on the seventh day and M. Mauriac is worrying, wondering and musing over his creation.

This is where things go wrong for him. He wrote once that the novelist was to his creatures what God was to His, and all the oddities of his technique can be explained by his taking the standpoint of God towards his characters. God sees the inside and the outside; he sees the depth of souls and bodies—the whole universe at a stroke. Similarly, M. Mauriac is omniscient about everything relating to his little world. What he says about his characters is the Gospel truth: he explains them, classifies them, condemns them unreservedly. If

---

21 Mauriac, *Thérèse*, p. 311.

you asked him, 'How do you know Thérèse is a cautious and desperate woman?' he would no doubt be amazed and would reply, 'Didn't I create her?'

Well, no, he didn't! The time has come to say that the novelist isn't God. Recall, rather, the precautions Conrad takes when suggesting to us that Lord Jim may perhaps be 'romantic'.[22] He is careful not to assert this himself, putting the word into the mouth of one of his creatures, a fallible human being who pronounces it hesitantly. Clear as it may be, the term 'romantic' is given depth, pathos and a hint of mystery. There is nothing of the sort with M. Mauriac. 'Cautious and desperate woman' isn't a hypothesis; it is a clear statement handed down from on high. Impatient to have us grasp the character of his heroine, the author suddenly provides us with the key. But I am arguing that he doesn't have the right to make these absolute judgements. A novel is an action related from various viewpoints. And M. Mauriac knows this well, writing as he does in *The End of the Night* that, 'one can make the most contrary judgements about the same person, and yet be right—that it is all a question of the way the light falls, and . . . no one form of lighting is more revealing than another.'[23] But each of these interpretations must be in motion; in other words, they must be carried along by the very

---

22 Joseph Conrad, *Lord Jim* (Edinburgh and London: William Blackwood and Sons, 1900). [Trans.]

23 Mauriac, *Thérèse*, p. 257.

action they are interpreting. Such an interpretation is, in short, the testimony of a participant, and it must reveal the person testifying as well as the event to which it testifies. It must arouse our impatience (will it be confirmed or refuted by events?) and in that way make us feel the resistance of time. Each point of view, then, is relative and the best will be of such a kind that time offers the reader the greatest resistance. The interpretations and explanations given by the participants will all be conjectural. Beyond these conjectures, the reader may perhaps sense an absolute reality of the event, but it is for him alone to establish this, if it suits him to do so, and, if he tries, he will never get beyond the realm of likelihoods and probabilities. In any event, the introduction of absolute truth or the viewpoint of God into a novel is a twofold technical error. First, it presupposes a narrator who is withdrawn from the action and purely contemplative, which offends against the aesthetic law, formulated by Paul Valéry, that any element of a work of art must always maintain a plurality of relations with the other elements. Second, the absolute is timeless. If you elevate the narrative into an absolute realm, the thread of time is broken and the novel vanishes before your very eyes. All that remains is a listless verity *sub specie aeternitatis*.

But there is something more serious. The definitive assessments M. Mauriac is always ready to slip into the narrative prove that he doesn't conceive his characters as he ought. He forges their essences before he writes; he decrees that they *will be* this or that. The essence of Thérèse, the evil-smelling animal or the cautious and desperate woman, is, I admit, complex, and not to be summed up in a single phrase. But what exactly is it? Her innermost depths? Let us take a close look at this. Conrad correctly saw that the word 'romantic' had meaning if it expressed an aspect of the character *for someone else.* Can we not see that 'cautious and desperate woman', 'evil-smelling animal', 'castaway' and all these neat little formulas are of the same kind as this little word that Conrad puts into the mouth of an inter-island merchant: they are the pithy turns of phrase of the moralist or the historian. And when Thérèse sums up her story ('As often as had been necessary . . . she . . . would drag herself out of the depths and then slip again to the bottom, and so on indefinitely, caught in the same weary process. For years she had not realized that this was to be the rhythm of her destiny, but now she had come through the dark night and could see her way clearly'),[24] she is able to judge her past so easily only because she cannot go back to it. In this way, M. Mauriac, when he believes he is probing into the depths of his characters, remains outside, at the door. There would be no problem if he realized this. In that case, he would gives us novels like Hemingway's, where we barely know the characters except through their actions and words and the vague judgements they pass on each other. But when

---

24 Mauriac, *Thérèse*, p. 256.

M. Mauriac, drawing on all his authority as creator, has us take these external views for the inner substance of his creations, he thereby transforms them into *things*. Except that things *are:* they have only exteriors. Minds cannot simply *be*: they *become*. Thus M. Mauriac, in sculpting his Thérèse *sub specie aeternitatis* turns her, first of all, into a thing. After which, he adds in a whole layer of consciousness below. But he does so in vain. Characters in novels have their laws and this is the strictest of them: the novelist may be their witness or their accomplice, but never both at the same time. Outside or inside. In failing to observe these laws, M. Mauriac slays the consciousnesses of his characters.

So we are brought back again to freedom, that other dimension of Thérèse. What becomes of her in this lifeless world? Up to now, Thérèse was a *thing* for us, an ordered succession of motifs and models, passions, habits and interests—a *story* we could sum up in a few maxims—*a fate*. And now suddenly, this witch, this possessed creature is presented to us as free. M. Mauriac is at pains to tell us what we are to understand by this particular kind of freedom:

> But what really gave me pleasure was that deci-
> sion I made yesterday to surrender my fortune.
> When I did that I felt as though I were floating
> at an incredible height above my *ordinary every-
> day self*. I climb and climb and climb—and then
> suddenly I slip back into this frozen nastiness of

malevolence—which is my true self when I'm not making an effort, *the self to which I keep on returning*.[25]

So her freedom no more constitutes Thérèse's 'real self' than did her consciousness. This self, 'which . . . I fall back to when I fall back to myself', is given in advance: it is the *thing*. Consciousness and freedom come afterwards, consciousness as a power to deceive oneself about oneself, freedom as a power to escape oneself. This means that, for M. Mauriac, freedom cannot *be constructive*. A human being cannot, with his freedom, create himself or forge his own history. Free will is merely a discontinuous power that enables one to escape from oneself for short periods, but produces nothing, except for a few inconsequential events. Hence, *The End of the Night*, which in M. Mauriac's eyes is supposed to be the novel of a character's freedom, seems to us chiefly to be a novel of bondage—to the point where the author, who initially wanted to show us 'the stages of a spiritual ascension', confesses in his preface that, against his will, Thérèse has dragged him down to Hell. 'Now that the story is finished,' he notes, not without regret, 'it has, to some extent, disappointed the hopes I had when I decided on its title.'[26] But how could it be otherwise? The very fact that the freedom is tacked on over and above the fixed, compact nature of Thérèse means it loses its omnipotence and

---

25 Mauriac, *Thérèse*, p. 218. My emphasis. [J.-P. S.]

26 Mauriac, *Thérèse*, p. 161.

indeterminacy; it receives a definition and a nature, since we know *what* it is a freedom *against*. More than this, indeed, M. Mauriac subjects it to a law: 'I climb and climb and climb—and then suddenly I slip back.' It is decreed in advance, then, that Thérèse will fall back each time. We are even warned in the preface that it would be indiscreet to ask more of her: 'She belongs to that class of human beings . . . for whom night can end only when life itself ends. All that is asked of them is that they should not resign themselves to night's darkness.'[27] And was it not Thérèse herself who was speaking, a moment ago, of the 'rhythm of her destiny': freedom is one of the phases of that rhythm. Thérèse is predictable even in her freedom. The little independence M. Mauriac grants her he has measured out precisely, as in a doctor's prescription or a recipe. I expect nothing from her; I know everything. Hence her ascents and falls move me little more than those of a cockroach mindlessly persisting in climbing a wall.

The point is that no scope has been left for freedom. Having been measured out with a pipette, Thérèse's freedom no more resembles real freedom than her consciousness resembles a real consciousness. And M. Mauriac, engrossed in describing Thérèse's psychological mechanisms, is suddenly at a loss when he wants to make us feel she is no longer a mechanism. Admittedly, he shows us Thérèse battling with her evil inclinations: 'Thérèse compressed her lips. "I won't tell her about that Garcin

---

27 Mauriac, *Thérèse*, p. 161.

creature," she kept saying to herself.'[28] But what is there to suggest that, behind this sudden revolt, a more thorough analysis wouldn't uncover the reasons and solid linkages of determinism? M. Mauriac is so acutely aware of this that, from time to time, he tugs at our sleeves and whispers to us, 'There you are, this time it's for real, she's free.' As in the following passage: 'She broke off in the middle of a sentence (for she was acting in entire good faith).'[29] I know of no cruder device than this parenthetical admonition. But we can understand why the author is bound to resort to it: if we start out from that hybrid being M. Mauriac has engendered and which he calls Thérèse's nature, *no sign could make the distinction between a free action and a passion.* Except perhaps for a kind of evanescent grace playing over the features or within the soul of a character who has just won a victory over him- or herself:

> Her gaze was as lovely as he had ever known it . . .[30]

> She felt no pang . . . Rather was she conscious of a sense of lightness. She seemed to have been freed by some *operation* of she knew not what. It was as though she were no longer walking in a circle, but moving straight ahead towards a goal.[31]

---

28 Mauriac, *Thérèse*, p. 217.
29 Mauriac, *Thérèse*, p. 240.
30 Mauriac, *Thérèse*, p. 258.
31 Mauriac, *Thérèse*, p. 199.

But these moral recompenses are not sufficient to convince us. They show us, rather, that for M. Mauriac freedom differs from bondage in its *value*, not its nature. Any intention directed upwards, towards Good, is free. Any desire for Evil is in bondage. The value of this distinguishing principle is not our concern here. The point is simply that it stifles novelistic freedom and, with it, the immediate *durée* that is the substance of the novel.

How could Thérèse's story *have duration*? We run up here against the old theological conflict between divine omniscience and human freedom: the 'rhythm of [Thérèse's] destiny', that graph of her rises and falls, resembles a temperature curve. We have before us dead time, since the future stretches out like the past, merely repeating it. The reader of the novel doesn't want to be God. For the transfusion of my own time into the veins of Thérèse and Marie Desqueyroux to take place, I would have to be—at least once—ignorant of their destinies and impatient to know about them. But M. Mauriac shows no concern to arouse impatience in me: his only aim is to provide me with as much knowledge as he possesses. He plies me with information, piling it on mercilessly. Barely has my curiosity been piqued than it is satisfied beyond all measure. Dostoevsky would have surrounded Thérèse with dense, secretive constructions, the meaning of which would have been on the point of revealing itself on every page, but would have eluded me. But right away M. Mauriac lodges me in the innermost hearts of his characters. No one has any secrets. An equal light is cast on all. So, even if, at times, I might have some appetite to know what happens next, I couldn't identify my impatience with Thérèse's, since we are not waiting for the same things and I have known the things she wants to know for quite some time. From my point of view, she is like those abstract partners in a 'demonstration hand' of bridge who are kept, hypothetically, in ignorance of their opponents' play and make their plans on the basis of that very ignorance, whereas I can see all the cards and can see that their calculations and hopes are erroneous; she is outside of my time, a fleshless shadow.

It is evident, moreover, that M. Mauriac doesn't at all like time or the Bergsonian necessity to wait 'for the sugar to melt'. His creatures' time is, for him, a dream, an all-too-human illusion. He casts it off and instals himself resolutely in the realm of the eternal. But, in my view, that alone should have deterred him from writing novels. The true novelist is excited by all that resists, by a door because it has to be opened, by an envelope because it has to be unsealed. In Hemingway's admirable *A Farewell to Arms*, things are time-traps. They provide the narrative with innumerable forms of trivial, but stubborn resistance, which the hero must break down one after the other. But M. Mauriac hates these tiny barriers that deflect him from his purpose; he speaks of them as little as possible. He even seeks to save time on his characters' conversations, taking over from them suddenly in mid-flow and summing up what they will say: 'Love,' said Thérèse,

is not the whole of life . . . not for men at least
. . .

She developed the theme at length. But had she
talked on until dawn the sound good sense
which she preached, from a feeling of duty and
not without effort, would have made no
impression whatever . . . etc.[32]

There is perhaps no graver error in the whole book
than these skimpings. By cutting short the dialogue of
his characters just as they are beginning to interest me,
M. Mauriac—how can he not see this?—suddenly bun-
dles me out of their time and out of their story. For these
dialogues don't come to an end. I know they carry on
somewhere, but I've merely been deprived of my right
to witness them. He would, no doubt, describe these
sudden stops, followed by equally sudden starts, as 'fore-
shortenings'. Personally, I would be inclined to term
them breakdowns. One has, admittedly, to 'foreshorten'
occasionally, but that doesn't mean one should suddenly
purge the narrative of its duration. In a novel, one must
either remain silent or tell all: one must, above all, not
omit or 'skip' anything. A foreshortening is simply a
gear-change in the narration. M. Mauriac, for his part,
is in a hurry. He has probably vowed that none of
his books will ever exceed the dimensions of a novella. I
have looked in vain in *The End of the Night* for those
long stammering conversations, so common in English

32 Mauriac, *Thérèse*, p. 249.

novels, in which the protagonists rake over their stories endlessly, without managing to get them forward, those periods of respite that suspend the action only to increase its urgency, those interludes in which, beneath a darkened sky, the characters are engrossed, like ants, in their familiar occupations. M. Mauriac will consent only to handling the essential passages, which he subsequently links together with brief summaries.

It is this taste for concision which explains why his creatures speak as if they are in the theatre. It is M. Mauriac's aim simply to have them express what they have to say as quickly and clearly as possible. Excluding superfluous detail, repetition and the stumblings of spoken language, he gives his protagonists' remarks their naked force of meaning. And since we have, nonetheless, to sense a difference between what he writes in his own name and what he makes them say, he imparts a kind of torrential speed to these excessively clear speeches that is, precisely, theatrical. This is Thérèse, for example:

> What are you trying to imply?—that I did not do what I say I did! It was evil, but nothing like so evil as my later crimes. They were more cowardly and more secret. With them I took no risks.[33]

This is a passage for recitation rather than for reading. Note the oratorical style of the beginning and the

---

33 Mauriac, *Thérèse*, p. 252.

repeated question that swells with the repetition. Doesn't it remind you of the rages of Hermione in Racine's *Andromaque*? I catch myself pronouncing the words *sotto voce*, in the grip of that rhetorical beginning that characterizes all good tragic dialogue. And now read this:

> However rash your friend may be, he cannot be
> so rash as to think you appeal to women. Had
> I meant to make him jealous, I should have
> shown greater regard for plausibility.[34]

Do you not recognize the turn of phrase so beloved of the comic writers of the eighteenth century? The novel is not at all suited to such airs and graces. It isn't that characters should speak as we do in life, but the novel has its own specific stylization. The transition to dialogue should be marked by a kind of dimming of the lights. It is dark, the hero struggles to express himself, his words are not pictures of his soul, but free, clumsy acts that say both too much and too little. The reader becomes impatient; he strives to see his way beyond these dense, stammered declarations. This resistance of words, the source of a thousand misunderstandings and of involuntary revelations, is something Dostoevsky, Conrad and Faulkner have been able to use to make dialogue that part of the novel in which time is at its densest. In his classicism, M. Mauriac no doubt finds such woolly conversations distasteful. But everyone

---

34 Mauriac, *La Fin de la Nuit*, p. 179. This passage is omitted from the edition used for the English translation. [Trans.]

knows that our classicism is a thing of oratory and theatricality.

This is not all. M. Mauriac demands that each of these conversations should be effective. In so doing, he is submitting again to a law of the theatre, for it is only in the theatre that dialogue must at all costs carry the action forward. As a result, he creates 'scenes'. The whole novel consists of four scenes, each of which ends in a 'catastrophe' and each of which is prepared with precision, as in a tragedy.

Judge by the following example. At Saint-Clair, Marie gets a letter from Georges, her fiancé, extricating himself from his engagement. Convinced, as a result of a misunderstanding, that her mother is responsible for the break-up, she sets out immediately for Paris. We have exact knowledge of this turbulent, selfish, passionate, rather stupid woman, who is capable of some good impulses. She is shown to us during the journey, mad with rage, her claws out, determined to fight, to do harm, to pay back her blows with interest. However, Thérèse's state is described to us just as precisely: we know her sufferings have undermined her health and she has suddenly gone half mad. Don't you see that the meeting between the two women is set up as in the theatre? We know the forces in play here, the situation is rigorously defined: this is a confrontation. Marie is unaware that her mother is mad; what will she do when she realizes? The problem is clearly formulated; determinism merely has to be left to run its course with its blows and counterblows, its predictable dramatic turnabouts. It will lead us, without fail, to the final catastrophe, with Marie transforming herself into a nursemaid and persuading her mother to come back to the Desqueyroux household. Is this not reminiscent of Sardou and the big scene in *L'Espionne*?[35] Or of Bernstein and the second act of *Le Voleur*?[36] I can quite understand M. Mauriac being tempted by the theatre: time and again, reading *The End of the Night*, I had the impression I was being presented with the plot and main extracts from a four-act play.

Look again now at the pages of *Beauchamp's Career* in which Meredith shows us the last meeting between Beauchamp and Renée: they are still in love and are within an ace of telling each other as much, and yet they separate.[37] When they meet, *everything* is possible between them; the future is not decided. Gradually, their tiny faults, their little misunderstandings and vexations begin to outweigh their goodwill. Their vision is clouded. And yet to the end, even as I am beginning to fear they will break up, I have a sense that *everything can still be different*. This is because they are free and they will themselves be the architects of their final separation. That is a novel.

---

35 Victorien Sardou (1831–1908): a prominent French dramatist. *L'Espionne* was a revised version of his play *Dora*, which had originally been produced at the Théâtre du Vaudeville in 1877. It was subsequently adapted for the English stage as *Diplomacy*. [Trans.]

36 Henri Bernstein (1876–1953): came to prominence thanks to the success of his play *Le Voleur* in 1906. [Trans.]

37 George Meredith, *Beauchamp's Career* (London: Oxford University Press, 1988). First published in 1876. [Trans.]

The End of the Night is not a novel. Are you going to call this angular, frosty work, with its theatrical passages, snippets of analysis and poetic meditations a novel? Can you mistake these jerky starts and equally violent applications of the brakes, these painful resumptions and breakdowns for the majestic course of novelistic time? Will you let your attention be grabbed by this static narrative, whose intellectual armature is visible at first glance, in which the mute figures of the protagonists are inscribed like angles within a circle? If it is the case that a novel is a *thing*, like a picture or an architectural creation, if it is the case that a novel is made with free minds and time, just as a picture is made with oil and pigments, then *The End of the Night* is not a novel. It is, at best, an assemblage of signs and intentions. M. Mauriac is not a novelist.

Why? Why has this serious, diligent author not reached his goal? The sin of pride is, I think, to blame. He has tried to ignore, as most of our authors do, that the theory of relativity applies fully to the universe of the novel; that in a genuine novel, as in Einstein's universe, there is no room for a privileged observer; and that in a novelistic system, as in a physical system, there is no experiment that enables us to detect whether that system is in motion or at rest.[38] M. Mauriac has put himself first. He has chosen divine omniscience and omnipotence. But

---

38 By 'novelistic system', I mean both the novel as a whole and the partial systems that make it up (the consciousnesses and the set of psychological and moral judgements of the characters).

GIDE ALIVE

We thought him sacred and embalmed: he dies and we discover how alive he still was; the unease and resentment that show through beneath the funerary wreaths so grudgingly woven for him demonstrate he still had the power to offend and will have for some time. He managed to unite right-thinking people of both Right and Left against him and you have only to imagine the joy of a few august old fogies as they exclaim, 'Thank you, Lord! So he really was in the wrong, since I'm the one who's still alive,' or to read, in *L'Humanité*, 'It is a corpse that has just died,' to see what an enormous influence this man of eighty, who had virtually given up writing, still had on the literature of our day.

There is a geography of thought. Just as a Frenchman, wherever he goes, cannot take a step on foreign soil without *also* moving closer to, or further from, France, so any step in our thinking *also* took us closer to Gide or further from him. His clarity, lucidity, rationalism and rejection of pathos gave others licence to venture into murkier, more uncertain, areas of thinking: one knew that, at the same time, a brilliant intelligence was upholding the rights of analysis, of purity and of a certain tradition. Had one foundered on one's voyage of discovery, one would not have dragged the mind down into the wreckage. The whole of French thought over the last thirty years, whether it liked it or not, and whatever its other points of reference—Marx, Hegel or Kierkegaard— had to define itself *also* in relation to Gide.

For my own part, the mental restrictions, the hypocrisy and, all in all, the contemptible foulness of the obituaries penned for him have annoyed me too much to contemplate setting down here what separated us from him. It is better to recall the inestimable gifts he bestowed on us.

I have learned from the pen of fellow journalists— who never struck me much by their boldness—that he 'lived dangerously beneath three layers of flannel'. What idiotic scoffing! These timorous creatures have invented a curious defence against the daring of others: they deign to acknowledge it only if it shows itself in all fields simultaneously. It seems Gide would have been forgiven for the risks he took with his thinking and reputation if he had also taken risks with his life and if, somewhat oddly, he had braved pneumonia. These people affect not to know that there are *different kinds* of courage and that they vary between people. Yes, Gide was cautious, he weighed his words, hesitated before signing anything, and, if he was interested in a movement of ideas or opinion, he saw to it that he gave it only conditional backing, remaining on the fringes, always ready to withdraw. But the same man dared to publish the profession of faith that is *Corydon*, the indictment that is *Travels in the Congo*,[1] and he had the courage to stand by the USSR when it was dangerous to do so and the greater courage publicly to reverse his opinion when he formed the view, rightly or wrongly, that he had been mistaken. It is perhaps this mix of wariness and audacity that makes him exemplary: generosity is a virtue only in those who know the price of things and, similarly, nothing is more moving than considered temerity. Written by an irresponsible person, *Corydon* would have been a mere moral scandal. But if its author is this wily, pernickety 'Oriental' who weighs everything, the book becomes a manifesto, a *testimony*, the significance of which goes far beyond the outrage it inspires. This wary audacity should be a 'Rule for the Guidance of the Mind': withhold one's judgement until the matter is clear and then, when one is firm in one's convictions, accept that one pays the price down to the very last penny.

Courage and caution: this judiciously balanced mixture explains the inner tension of his work. Gide's art seeks to strike a compromise between risk and rule. In him are balanced the Protestant law and the nonconformity of the homosexual; the proud individualism of the *grand bourgeois* and the Puritanical preference for social constraint; a certain curtness of manner, a difficulty in communicating and a humanism of Christian origin; a lively sensuality and yet a view of that sensuality as innocent. Observance of the rule is united here with the quest for spontaneity. This balancing act underlies the inestimable service Gide rendered contemporary literature: he it was who lifted it out of the symbolist rut. The second symbolist generation had convinced themselves that the writer demeaned himself if he ventured beyond a very narrow range of subjects, all of them very elevated, but that he could, on these clearly defined subjects, express himself in any manner he wished. Gide freed us from this naïve focus on subject matter: he taught us, or re-taught us, that *anything* could be said— that was his audacity—but according to certain rules of literary elegance—that was his caution.

From this cautious audacity came his perpetual turnabouts, his oscillations from one extreme to the other, his passion for objectivity, for what one should even term his 'objectivism'—a highly bourgeois characteristic, I admit—that made him look for Reason and for the right even in his opponent's positions and saw him fascinated by the opinions of others. I do not claim at all that these attitudes, so characteristic of the man, could serve us well today, but they enabled him to make his life a strictly conducted experiment that we can assimilate without any preparation; in a word, he *lived* his ideas. And one in particular: the death of God. I do not imagine that a single believer today was led to Christianity by the arguments of St Bonaventure or St Anselm, but I don't believe either that a single non-believer was turned from the faith by the opposite arguments. The problem of God is a human problem that concerns the relationships of human beings among themselves; it is a total problem to which everyone brings a solution by their whole life, and the solution one brings reflects the attitude one has chosen towards other human beings and oneself. The most precious thing Gide offers us is his decision to live out to the end the agony and death of God. He could, like so many others, have taken a gamble on concepts, plumped for faith or atheism at the age of twenty and held to that throughout his life. Instead of so doing, he wanted to *test out* his relation to religion, and the living dialectic that led him to his ultimate atheism is a path others can follow in his footsteps but not one that can be fixed in concepts or notions.

His interminable discussions with the Catholics, his outpourings, shafts of irony, flirtations, sudden breaks, advances, spells of marking time, backslidings, the ambiguity of the word 'God' in his work, his refusal to abandon it even when he believed only in humanity—all this rigorous experimentation has, in fact, done more to enlighten us than a hundred demonstrations. He lived *for us* a life we have only to relive by reading him; he

✳

PORTRAIT OF A MAN UNKNOWN

One of the oddest features of our literary age is the appearance here and there of enduring, totally negative works that might be termed anti-novels. I shall place the works of Nabokov in this category, together with those of Waugh and, in a sense, Gide's *Counterfeiters*.[1] These are not essays attacking the novel genre, such as *Puissances du roman* by Caillois,[2] which I would compare, with all due allowances, to Rousseau's *Lettre sur les spectacles*.[3] Anti-novels retain the appearance and outlines

---

1 André Gide, *Les faux-monnayeurs* (1925); first published in *Nouvelle Revue Française*; *The Counterfeiters* (Dorothy Bussy trans.) (New York: Alfred A. Knopf, 1927). [Trans.]

2 Robert Caillois, *Puissances du roman* (Marseille: Sagittaire, 1942). [Trans.]

3 Jean-Jacques Rousseau, *Lettre à M. d'Alembert sur les Spectacles* (1758)—a refutation of d'Alembert's article 'Genève' in Denis Diderot and Jean le Rond d'Alembert (eds), *Encyclopédie ou Dictionnaire raisonné des sciences, des arts et des métiers* (Paris: 1751–77, 32 vols), VOL. 7 (1757), p. 578. [Trans.]

of the novel; they are works of the imagination that present us with fictional characters and tell us their story. But they do so only the better to deceive: the aim is to use the novel to contest the novel; to destroy it before our eyes as it is apparently being constructed; to write the novel of a novel that does not become one, that cannot become one; to create a fiction that is to the great compositions of Dostoyevsky and Meredith what Miró's canvas, *The Murder of Painting* [*El asesinato de la pintura*], is to the pictures of Rembrandt and Rubens. These strange works, which are difficult to classify, do not attest to the weakness of the novel genre, but merely indicate that we are living through a period of reflection and that the novel is currently reflecting on itself. Nathalie Sarraute's is a novel of this kind: it is an anti-novel that reads like a detective story. It is, indeed, a parody of the 'quest novel' and she has introduced into it a kind of impassioned amateur detective who is fascinated by a quite ordinary couple, an ageing father and a daughter no longer very young; he spies on them, tails them and sometimes remotely divines their thoughts by a kind of mental transference, but without ever knowing very clearly what he is after nor who they are. And indeed he will find nothing, or *almost* nothing. He will abandon his investigation as a result of a metamorphosis: as though Agatha Christie's detective, on the point of unmasking the villain, suddenly turned criminal.

It is the bad faith of the novelist—that *necessary* bad faith—that horrifies Nathalie Sarraute. Is he 'with' his characters, 'behind' them or outside? And when he is behind them, does he not try to convince us that he remains inside or outside? Through the fiction of this soul-detective, who hits up against the 'outside', against the shells of these 'enormous dung-beetles' and dimly senses the 'inside' without ever touching it, Nathalie Sarraute seeks to preserve her good faith as a storyteller. She does not want to come at her characters from either the inside or the outside, because we are—for ourselves and for others—wholly outside and inside at one and the same time. The outside is a neutral ground; it is this *inside* of ourselves that we want to be for others and that others encourage us to be for ourselves. This is the realm of the *commonplace*. And this fine word has several meanings: it refers, doubtless, to the most hackneyed of thoughts, but these thoughts have become the meeting-place of the community. Everyone finds himself in them and finds the others too. The commonplace is everyone's and it belongs to me; it belongs in me to everyone and it is the presence of everyone in me. It is, in its essence, *generality*; to appropriate it requires an act: an act by which I strip away my particularity in order to adhere to the general, to become generality. Not in any sense *similar* to everyone, but, to be precise, the *incarnation* of everyone. By this eminently social adherence, I identify myself with *all* others in the indistinctness of the universal.

Nathalie Sarraute seems to distinguish three concentric spheres of generality: the sphere of character, the sphere of the moral commonplace and the sphere of art, which precisely includes the novel. If I act the kindly rough diamond, like the old father in *Portrait of a Man Unknown*,[4] I confine myself to the first sphere. If, when a father refuses to give his daughter money, I declare: 'How sad to see that. And to think she's all he has in the world . . . Ah, he can't take it with him now, can he?' I project myself into the second. If I describe a young woman as a Tanagra, a landscape as a Corot or a family story as being like a Balzac novel, then I move into the third. The others, who have easy access to these domains, approve and understand right away; by reflecting my attitude, judgement or comparison, they impart a sacred character to it. This is reassuring for others and reassuring for myself, since I have taken refuge in this neutral, common zone that is neither entirely objective—since I am there by decree—nor entirely subjective—because everyone can reach me and be at home there—but may be termed both the subjectivity of the objective and the objectivity of the subjective. As I claim to be nothing other than this, and protest that I have no hidden dimensions, I am permitted, at this level, to chatter away, to be stirred or even indignant, to show 'a character', even to be 'an eccentric'—in other words, to assemble commonplaces in an unprecedented way: there is even such a thing as the 'common paradox'. All in all, I am

4 Nathalie Sarraute, *Portrait d'un inconnu* (Paris: Robert Marin, 1948; first edition); *Portrait of a Man Unknown* (Maria Jolas trans.) (New York: Braziller, 1958). [Trans.]

free to be subjective within the limits of objectivity. And the more subjective I am within these narrow bounds, the more I will be thanked for it, since I shall show thereby that the subjective is nothing and one should not be afraid of it.

In her first work, *Tropisms*, Nathalie Sarraute showed us how women spend their lives *communing* in the commonplace:

> They talked: 'They have awful scenes about nothing at all. I must say that he's the one I feel sorry for in it all. How much? Oh, at least two million. And if only what she inherited from her Aunt Josephine . . . No . . . How could it? He won't marry her. What he needs is a good housewife . . . Housewife . . . Housewife . . .' They had always heard it said, they knew it: the sentiments, love, life, these were their domain. It belonged to them.[5]

This is Heidegger's 'chatter', the realm of his impersonal *das Man* (the 'they') and, in a word, of inauthenticity. And many authors have no doubt brushed against or scraped along the wall of inauthenticity, but I know none who have deliberately made it the subject of a book: the fact is that inauthenticity is not novelistic. Novelists strive, rather, to persuade us that the world is made up

---

5 Nathalie Sarraute, *Tropismes* (first edition: Paris: Denoël, 1939); *Tropisms* (Maria Jolas trans.) (London: John Calder, 1963). [Trans.]

of irreplaceable individuals, all of them exquisite, even the wicked ones, all of them passionate and individual. Nathalie Sarraute shows us the wall of the inauthentic; she shows it to us everywhere. And what is there behind this wall? Well, there is precisely *nothing*. Or almost nothing. Vague efforts to evade something one divines in the shadows. *Authenticity*, a real relationship with others, with oneself, with death, is everywhere suggested, but remains invisible. We sense it because we flee it. If, as the author invites us, we take a glance inside people, we glimpse a teeming sprawl of spineless evasions of authenticity. There is the escape into objects that peacefully reflect permanence and the universal, the escape into daily occupations, the escape into pettiness. I know of few more impressive pages than those that show us 'the old man' only just managing to escape the panic fear of death by charging, barefooted in his nightshirt, into the kitchen to check whether his daughter is stealing soap from him. Nathalie Sarraute has a protoplasmic view of our inner world: roll away the stone of the commonplace and you find flows of liquid, trickles of slobber, mucus, and hesitant, amoeboid movements. She has an incomparably rich vocabulary for suggesting the slow centrifugal reptations of these viscous, living elixirs. '[L]ike some sort of sticky slaver, their thought filtered in to him, lined him internally.' And here we have the pure girl-woman: 'sitting silent in the lamplight, looking like some frail, gentle under-seas plant, entirely lined with mobile suckers . . .'[6] The fact is that these stumbling, shameful evasions that dare not speak their name are also relations with others. Thus, hallowed conversation, that ritual exchange of commonplaces, conceals a 'half-voiced conversation' in which the suckers brush up against each other, lick and suck each other. There is, first, a sense of *unease*: if I suspect that you *are not* quite simply, quite plainly the commonplace you *utter*, then all my formless monsters are roused and I am afraid:

> She was sitting crouched on a corner of the chair, squirming, her neck outstretched, her eyes bulging: 'Yes, yes, yes, yes,' she said, and she confirmed each part of the sentence with a jerk of her head. She was frightening, mild and flat, quite smooth, and only her eyes were bulging. There was something distressing, disquieting about her and her mildness was threatening.
>
> He felt that she should be set straight, soothed, at any cost, but that only someone endowed with superhuman strength would be able to do it . . . He was afraid, he was on the verge of panic, he must not waste a second trying to reason it out, to think. And, as usual, as soon as he saw her, he assumed the role that, through compulsion, through threats, it seemed to him she forced him to assume. He started to talk, to talk without stopping, about just

6 Sarraute, *Portrait of a Man Unknown*, p. 30. [Trans.]

anybody, just anything, tossing from side to side (like a snake at the sound of music? like birds in the presence of a boa? he no longer knew). He must hurry, hurry, without stopping, without a minute to lose, hurry, hurry while there's still time, to restrain her, to placate her.[7]

Nathalie Sarraute's books are full of these terrors: people are talking, something is about to explode, is about to illuminate suddenly the murky depths of a soul, and everyone will feel the shifting mire of his own. And then, no: the threat averted, the danger avoided, it is back to trading commonplaces again. Yet, at times these break down and a horrible, protoplasmic nudity appears:

> It seemed to them that their outlines were breaking up, stretching in every direction, their carapaces and armours seemed to be cracking on every side, they were naked, without protection, they were slipping, clasped to each other, they were going down as into the bottom of a well . . . down where they were going now, things seemed to wobble and sway as in an undersea landscape, at once distinct and unreal, like objects in a nightmare, or else they became swollen, took on strange proportions . . . a great flabby mass was weighing on her, crushing her

---

7 Sarraute, *Portrait of a Man Unknown*, p. 30. [Trans.]

. . . she tried clumsily to disengage herself a bit,
she heard her own voice, a funny, too neutral-
sounding voice.[8]

In fact, nothing happens: nothing ever happens.
With one accord, the interlocutors draw a veil of generality over this transient moment of weakness. So we
should not look to Nathalie Sarraute's book for what she
is not trying to give us; for her, a human being isn't a
character or, primarily, a history or even a skein of habits,
but the ceaseless, flabby toing-and-froing between the particular and the general. Sometimes the shell is empty; a
'Monsieur Dumontet' comes in suddenly; having artfully
sloughed off all particulars, he is merely a charming,
lively assemblage of generalities. Everyone then breathes
easily and recovers hope: it was possible, after all! It is,
after all, still possible. A deathly calm accompanies him
into the room.

These few remarks are meant merely to guide the
reader through this excellent, difficult book; they are not
intended as an exhaustive treatment of its content. The
best thing about Nathalie Sarraute is her stumbling,
groping style, so honest and full of misgivings; it comes
at its object with pious precautions, sidesteps it suddenly
out of a kind of modesty or timidity at the complexity
of things and, in the end, presents us suddenly with the
drooling monster, but almost without having touched
it, doing so merely by the magic of an image. Is this

8 Sarraute, *Portrait of a Man Unknown*, p. 57.

psychology? Perhaps Nathalie Sarraute, a great admirer of Dostoyevsky, wants to persuade us that it is. For my part, I believe that, by allowing us to sense an elusive authenticity, by showing this incessant toing-and-froing from the particular to the general, by tenaciously depicting the reassuring, desolate world of the inauthentic, she has developed a technique that enables her to attain, beyond psychology, human reality in its very *existence.*

Preface to Nathalie Sarraute, *Portrait d'un Inconnu* (Paris: Gallimard, 1957).

*

MONSIEUR JEAN GIRAUDOUX AND THE PHILOSOPHY OF ARISTOTLE: ON *CHOIX DES ÉLUES*

Everything we are able to know of Monsieur Giraudoux suggests that he is 'normal' in both the most common-place and the most elevated sense of the term. Further-more, his critical studies have enabled us to appreciate the supple delicacy of his intelligence. However, as soon as you open one of his novels, you have the impression of entering the universe of one of those waking dreamers, known medically as 'schizophrenics', who are character-ized, as we know, by an inability to adapt themselves to reality. The main characteristics of these patients—their stiffness, their efforts to deny change and to mask the pre-sent, their geometrism, their taste for symmetry, general-izations, symbols and magical correspondences across time and space—are all taken on by M. Giraudoux and artfully developed: it is in them that the charm of his book resides. I have often been intrigued by the contrast between the man and his work. Might it be that M. Giraudoux finds entertainment in playing the schizophrenic?

Choix des Élues, which was serialized in this very publication,[1] seemed valuable to me because it provided me with an answer. It is probably not M. Giraudoux's best book. But precisely because many of the charms of his style have turned into devices in it, it is easier to grasp the turn of this strange mind. It became clear to me, first of all, that I had been kept from the true interpretation of his work by a prejudice I must share with many of his readers. Up to now, I have always attempted to *translate* his books. In other words, I have acted as though M. Giraudoux had amassed a great many observations and had derived a particular wisdom from them and had then, out of fondness for a certain preciosity, expressed all this experience and wisdom in coded language. My attempts at decipherment had never produced any great results. M. Giraudoux's profundity is genuine, but it is a profundity for his world, not for ours. So on this occasion I did not try to translate, I did not seek out the metaphor, the symbol or the hidden meaning. I took everything at face value with the aim of increasing, not my knowledge of human beings, but my knowledge of M. Giraudoux. To enter fully the universe of *Choix des*

---

1 *La Nouvelle Revue Française*, March 1940. [J.-P. S.] [The book itself, *Choix des Élues*, was published by Grasset (Paris) in 1939. (Trans.)]

Élues, we must first forget the world in which we live. I therefore pretended I knew nothing of our doughy world, rippled by waves whose causes and ends originate elsewhere, nothing of our futureless world made up solely of fresh encounters, in which the present breaks in like a thief, events naturally resist thought and language, and individuals are accidents, lumps of grit, for which the mind retrospectively devises general headings.

I was not wrong to do so. In the America of Edmée, Claudie and Pierre, order and intelligible states of rest exist first; they are the goal of change and its only justification. I was struck from the beginning of the book by these clear little states of rest; the book is made up of rests. A jar of gherkins is not the chance aspect assumed by circling atoms, it is a state of rest, a form closed in upon itself; the mind of a graduate of *Polytechnique*, stuffed with calculations and entitlements, is another state of rest; and rest too is the light head of a painter in the lap of a beautiful, motionless woman—or a landscape, a public park or even the fleeting impression of a morning. These boundaries or limits assigned to the becoming of matter we shall call, as they did in the Middle Ages, 'substantial forms'. M. Giraudoux is so constituted that he first grasps the species in the individual and the thought in matter: 'A truth that was Edmée's face,' he writes. Things are like that in his universe: they are truths first, ideas first, meanings that choose their signs for themselves. 'Jacques, *like an artless little boy*, reticent in his joy and his sorrow alike, had immediately diverted

familiar devices. But the disrespect he shows here for the established order has meaning only in relation to that order itself. With M. Giraudoux, as in the wisdom of the old saw, the exception is only there to prove the rule.

We should not believe, however, that M. Giraudoux espouses Platonism. His forms are not to be found in the heaven of ideas, but among us; they are inseparable from the matter whose movements they regulate; impressed, like seals in glass or steel, upon our skins. Nor should they be confused with mere concepts. Concepts contain barely any more than a handful of characteristics common to all the individuals in a group. In truth M. Giraudoux's forms contain no more than that, but all their constitutive features are perfect. Rather than mere general ideas, they are norms and canons. Without a doubt, Jacques spontaneously applies off his own bat all the rules enabling him to achieve, within himself, the perfection of the artless little boy. And the very movement that brought Pierre into being made him the most perfect realization of the Polytechnique-educated husband. 'Edmée's canines, *so distinctly canine . . .*' writes M. Giraudoux. And, further on: 'In order to watch over his mother, Jacques had assumed the tenderest form of Jacques.' And again: 'The annoying thing about Pierre was that he had made such efforts to be representative of humanity that he had genuinely become so. Each of his actions and each of his utterances was now merely the attested sample of human action and language.' It is the same with all of the entities in M. Giraudoux's work: his books are samplings. When questioned by Parmenides, Socrates was reluctant to admit that there was an Idea of dirt, an Idea of the louse. M. Giraudoux wouldn't hesitate. The lice he deals with have the admirable quality of each being the perfection of the louse—all of them equally, though in diverse ways. This is why, rather than the name concept, these substantial forms would deserve that of archetype, and our author does sometimes use this himself: '(Pierre looks at Edmée and) draws back to see only the archetype of Edmée.' But there are also individual perfections. Edmée, who is certainly the most distinctly motherly of mothers—like all mothers—and the most distinctly wifely wife—like all wives—is also most distinctly and perfectly Edmée. And even among the gherkins which, for the most part, limit themselves resignedly to realizing the consummate type of the gherkin, a few rare, privileged ones are nevertheless endowed with a singular archetypal character:

> She went to fetch a gherkin. Though one does not choose gherkins, she obeyed him, taking the one which, by its architecture, sculpture and relief could claim the title of head of household's gherkin.

We can see what the world of *Choix des Élues* is like: it is a botanical atlas, in which all the species are carefully classified, in which the periwinkle is blue because it is a periwinkle and the oleanders are pink because they are pink oleanders. The only causality is that of archetypes. There is no place in this world for determinism, the causative action of anterior states. But you won't find any *events* there either, if by 'event' one means the irruption of a new phenomenon, whose very novelty exceeds all expectation and overturns the order of concepts. There is hardly any change here, except for that of matter being acted upon by form. And the action of this form is of two kinds. It may act by *innate potentiality*, like fire in the Middle Ages which burned thanks to phlogiston: in that case, it implants itself in the matter, shapes it and moves it at will. Movement is then merely the temporal development of the archetype. In this way, most of the actions in *Choix des Élues* are the actions of people possessed. Characters by their acts, and things by their changes, merely realize their substantial forms the more closely:

> No peril hovered around these heads. They were resplendent. They signalled to happiness like beacons, *each with its own lighting system*; Pierre, the husband, with his two smiles, one big, one small, which followed within a second of each other every minute; Jacques, the son, with his face itself, which he raised and lowered, Claudie, the daughter, a more sensitive beacon, with the fluttering of her eyelids.

In this sense, the various alterations of this universe, which we must reluctantly agree to call events, are always the symbols of the forms producing them. But the form may also act by elective affinity. Hence the title *Choix des Élues* (Choice of the Elect). At bottom, every one of M. Giraudoux's creatures is a member of the 'elect'. This is because a form, lurking in the future, lies in wait for its matter. It has chosen it and attracts it to itself. And the second kind of change is of this order: a rapid transition from one form to the other; a becoming that is narrowly defined by its point of origin and its point of arrival. The bud is repose and so too is the flower. Between the two states of rest there is an oriented alteration, the only contingency in this ordered world, a necessary and inexpressible evil. Of this process of becoming, itself, there is nothing to say and M. Giraudoux speaks of it as little as possible. Yet the subject of *Choix des Élues* is a process of becoming. That subject is the becoming of Edmée, the Chosen One. But M. Giraudoux gives us merely its successive stages. Each of his chapters is a 'stasis'; Edmée at her birthday dinner, Edmée in the night, a description of Claudie, Edmée at Frank's, motionless, supporting the weight of a 'light head' on her lap. Edmée at the public park, which is 'outside time', Edmée at the Leeds', etc. The transitions occur off stage, like the murders in Corneille. We are now able to understand that semblance of schizophrenia that had struck us at the outset in Giraudoux's world: it is a world without present indicative. This noisy, shapeless present of surprises and catastrophes has lost its gravity and sparkle; it goes by very quickly and tactfully, excusing itself as it passes.

Admittedly, there are, here and there, a few scenes and actions that 'take place', a few adventures that 'occur'. But all that is already more than half generalized away, for the main thing is to describe the symbols of certain archetypes. We repeatedly lose our purchase as we read, sliding imperceptibly from present individuality to timeless forms. At no point do we *feel* the weight of this head lying in Edmée's lap, at no point do we see it in its charming, frivolous individuality, in the light of an American spring. But this is of no importance, since the only concern is to determine whether it is in the nature of a Polytechnic graduate's head to be heavier than the crazy head of an artist. The point is that there are two presents in M. Giraudoux's work: the shameful present of the event, which is concealed as much as possible, like some hereditary defect, and the present of archetypes, which is eternity.

These perpetual limitations of the process of becoming naturally accentuate the discontinuous character of time. Since change is a lesser entity, which exists only for the purpose of rest, time is merely a succession of little jolts, an arrested film. Here is how Claudie thinks of her past:

> There had been a series of a hundred or a thousand little girls that had succeeded each other day by day to produce the Claudie of today . . . She gathered together the photographs of this multitude of Claudies, of Claudettes, Claudines

and Clo-Clos—there had been a Clo-Clo the country girl for six months—not as photographs of her, but as family portraits.

This is the temporality of *Choix des Élues:* that of the family album. You have to turn the pages, but that is nothing but a little, unremembered disorder between the calm dignity of two portraits.

This is what explains M. Giraudoux's penchant for first beginnings. 'For the first time . . .', 'It was the first time . . .'—perhaps no other phrase recurs so frequently in his work. And perhaps never so frequently as in *Choix des Élues* (see, for example, pages 16, 32, 58, 59, 66, 68, 83, 86, etc.). This is because forces in M. Giraudoux's world are oblivious of progression. In our world, we question the past and seek in vain after origins: 'When did I begin to love her?' To tell the truth, this love never began: it came into being little by little and when I eventually discovered my passion, its freshness was already gone. But in M. Giraudoux, changes are instantaneous, since they obey the famous 'all or nothing' principle. When the conditions are in place, the form appears suddenly and embeds itself in the matter. But if one factor is missing—a single, minuscule factor— nothing happens. Thus our reading carries us, from beginning to beginning, through an awakening world. If we may speak of an atmosphere common to *Simon Le Pathétique, Églantine* and *Jérome Bardini*, it is surely that of morning. From one end of these books to the other, despite ageing and nightfalls, and even massacres, the sun rises. *Électre* closes on a catastrophe and a dawn. Shall I dare say, however, that, reading *Choix des Élues*, I no longer had the impression of those charming daybreaks that Jérôme and Bella chose for their meetings? It seemed to me I was condemned to an eternal morning.

Like the beginnings, the endings are absolute. When the balance is disrupted, the form disappears as it arrived—discreetly, totally: 'In the early morning, Edmée was there without a wrinkle or a smudge on her face, and the long night that had just passed even seemed to have been subtracted from her age.' Marks, wrinkles, blemishes—these are things that properly belong in our world. But M. Giraudoux's world is a world of reconquered virginities. His creatures share a metaphysical chastity. They do, admittedly, make love. But neither love nor motherhood leave a mark on them. The nudity of his women is, admittedly, 'most distinctly nudity'. They are nudes and nothing but nudes; absolutely and perfectly nude, without any of the birthmarks, swellings and subsidings that have no part in the archetype of the nude. Like those film stars Jean Prévost called 'gloveskin women', they have bodies scoured like Dutch kitchens and their flesh gleams with the freshness of scrubbed tiles.

And yet this orderly house stands under the laws of magic. Or, rather, of alchemy, since we find strange transmutations there, in the sense in which the Middle Ages spoke of the transmutation of metals, and of strange remote influences. 'The first week of Claudie's life was the first week Edmée knew a world without spiders, without banana skins, without hairdressers with excessively hot curling tonguess.' Edmée, who is soon going to leave her husband, lies beside him in an off-cream nightdress with Valenciennes lace and a yoke. The objects in the bedroom grew angry and insulted her. She bounded into the bathroom and put on a pair of Pierre's pyjamas.

> The bed fell silent . . . And so the night passed. In these two similar articles of clothing, they seemed to form a team. Those who can see in the dark would have taken them for twins or a matching pair. Deceived by this sudden mimicry, the objects gradually quietened down . . .

And here we have the description of an exorcism:

> Disguised as Claudie, those who wanted to give Edmée white hair, loose teeth and hard skin tried to get into the bed from the space between it and the wall. She had to accept their convention, take them by Claudie's hand, take them back to Claudie's bed and threaten Claudie with no dessert for a week. God knows they didn't care! But, bound by their disguise, they had to obey.

All that is needed, then, to exorcise the demons that have taken on Claudie's shape, is to treat them *as* Claudie.

What does all this mean? M. Giraudoux explains it to us himself:

> With Claudie, *everything that resembled* Claudie in this lowly world approved of her . . . Her peace with little Claudie was peace with all that is not commonplace, with all that is great, with the mineral and the vegetal, with all that endures.

This is the characteristic feature of all enchantments and spells: resemblance exerts an effect. But we should be clear here that in Giraudoux resemblance is not a perception of the mind: it is *realized*. The 'like' which he employs so generously is never intended to clarify: it marks a substantial analogy between acts and between things. We should not, however, be surprised by this, since M. Giraudoux's universe is a Natural History. In his eyes, objects are in some sense similar when, in some aspect or other, they share in the same form. It is, of course, only with Claudie that Edmée is seeking peace. But Claudie is, precisely, that which 'is not commonplace'. To make peace with Claudie is to adapt oneself more closely to the form she currently embodies, to the form of 'all that is great . . . all that endures'. So, by approaching, out of love for Claudie, the perishable incarnation of an eternal archetype, Edmée finds herself thereby mysteriously in tune with all the incarnations of that archetype: with the desert, the mountains and the virgin forest. But this is *logical* once we take into account that Edmée has attuned herself, once and for all, to a universal form. The magic is merely an appearance, arising from the fact that this form is refracted through countless particles of matter. Hence these deep analogies that M. Giraudoux likes to point up between the most diverse objects: the presence of forms divides the universe into an infinity of infinite regions and, in each of these regions, any old object, if we question it in the right way, tells us about all the others. In each of these regions, to love, hate or insult any object is to insult, love and hate all the others. Analogies, correspondences, symbolisms—these are what constitute the marvellous for M. Giraudoux. But, like mediaeval magic, all this is merely a strict application of the logic of the concept.

We have here then a ready-made world, a world that is not in the making. The world of Linnaeus, not of Lamarck. The world of Cuvier, not of Geoffroy Saint-Hilaire. Let us ask now what place M. Giraudoux reserves in it for man. We can sense that it is sizeable. If we remind ourselves that in this world magic is merely an appearance, that it is due simply to a hyperlogicism, we shall first have to record that this world is, to its very core, accessible to reason. M. Giraudoux has banished from it all that might surprise or disconcert us: development, becoming, disorder and novelty. Surrounded by ready-made thoughts, by the reason of trees and stones, the reason of moon and water, man has no other concern than to enumerate and contemplate. And I imagine M.

Giraudoux himself has a fondness for the functionaries in the Registry Office: the writer, as he conceives him, is merely a clerk in the Land Registry. And yet a rational world could still be a source of anxiety: think of Pascal's infinite spaces or Vigny's Nature. But there is nothing of that kind here: there is a close affinity between man and world. Remember Claudie and her resemblance to the desert or the virgin forest. Can you not see that the toughness, the strength, the eternity of a forest or desert is also the eternity in the moment, the gentle strength, the frail toughness of a little girl? Humanity finds all the archetypes of nature within itself and, conversely, it finds itself in all of nature. It stands at the crossroads of all 'regions'; it is the centre of the world and a symbol of the world, like the microcosm of the magicians within the great Cosmos. Let us note that the human being, who is so well ensconced in the universe and feels at home everywhere, has not been subjected by M. Giraudoux to the influence of determinism. His character is not the outcome of a thousand imponderables, of his history or his stomach troubles. His character in no way forms as time progresses. On the contrary, it is his history—and even his stomach troubles—that are the products of his character. This is what is called 'having a destiny'. Consider, for example, the terms Edmée uses to warn her young son against love:

> Oh, little Jacques, haven't you seen yourself? Look at yourself in a mirror. It's not that you're

bad looking, but you'll see you're a born victim,
a ready-made victim . . . You've got just the kind
of face for tears, with your head pressed into the
pillow, the sort of cheeks for sinking into hands
that tremble with despair, the kind of tall body
that waits on street corners in the rain . . . the
breastbone of those who sob without resorting
to tears . . .

For Giraudoux, the character of a human being is
not really different from the 'essence' of the gherkin: it
is an archetype realized by way of human life through
human acts; an archetype for which the human body is
the perfect symbol. In this way, through symbols, the
most perfect union between mind and body is achieved:
the path is open to characterology, to the judgement of
character from the face. But if we have swapped the psy-
chologist's determinism for the logical necessity of
essences, we don't seem to have gained much in the
exchange. Admittedly, there is no longer any psychology,
if by that we mean a set of empirically observed laws gov-
erning the course of our moods. But we haven't chosen
what we are; we are 'possessed' by a form. There is nothing we can do about it. However, we are now protected
from universal determinism: there is no danger of our
being diluted into the universe. The human being is a
finite, *defined* reality and not in any sense an effect produced by the world or a by-product of blind chains of
causation. He is a 'man' or a 'Polytechnique-educated

husband' or 'a young boy born to suffer for love' in the same way as a circle is a circle. And, for this reason, he is at the origin of first beginnings: his acts emanate from himself alone. Is this freedom? It is, at least, a *certain kind* of freedom. Moreover, it seems M. Giraudoux confers another kind on his creations: man *spontaneously* realizes his essence. For the mineral and vegetal realms, conformity is automatic. Man, by contrast, conforms to his archetype by an act of will; he perpetually *chooses himself* as he *is*. This is, admittedly, a one-way freedom, for if the form is not   realized *by* him, it will be realized *through* him and without him. To appreciate the fineness of the line between this freedom and absolute necessity, compare the following two passages. Here is freedom, inspiration:

> Where can we go, Claudie, where we've never been before?'
>
> 'To Washington Park.'
>
> Claudie never hesitated. For every question, even the most embarrassing, she had a ready answer . . . What a happy inspiration to have chosen to come here the very time when parks are useless to humans.

As we can see, there was intuition in this, the poetic creation of an accord between the two women and inanimate objects. But in that very intuition, Claudie couldn't help realizing her essence. She is 'the one who never hesitates'. It was part of her essence to have this intuition. And here, now, is a case where the harmony between our archetype and the world manifests itself through us, without asking our opinion:

> Edmée was amazed at the words that came to her own lips, for they were surprising. But she was *even more amazed at the necessity of what she said* than at its monstrousness.

The difference is not great: in the one case, the form realizes itself through our will; in the other, it spreads through our bodies as though of its own accord. And yet this is what separates man from the gherkin. This fragile, intermittent freedom, which isn't an end in itself but merely a means, is enough to confer a duty upon us. M. Giraudoux has a morality. Man must realize his finite essence freely and thereby attune himself freely to the rest of the world. Every man is responsible for the universal harmony; he must submit himself willingly to the necessity of the archetypes. And at the very moment this harmony appears, when this balance emerges between our deepest inclinations, between nature and spirit, at the moment when man is at the centre of an ordered world, when he is 'most distinctly' man at the centre of a world that is 'most distinctly' world, M. Giraudoux's creation receives his reward. That reward is happiness. And here we see what this author's famous humanism amounts to: a pagan eudaemonism.

A concept-based philosophy, scholastic problems (is it form or matter that individualizes?), a shamefaced conception of becoming, defined as the transition from potential to act, a white magic that is merely the superficial aspect of a rigorous logicism, a morality of equilibrium, happiness and the golden mean—this is what we get from a candid examination of *Choix des Élues*. We are a long way here from waking dreamers. But there is an even stranger surprise in store: for in these few characteristic traits we cannot fail to recognize the philosophy of Aristotle. Wasn't it Aristotle who was first a logician—and a logician of the concept, and a magician through logic? Isn't it in his work that we find this tidy, finite, hierarchized world, that is rational to the core. Isn't he the one who sees knowledge as contemplation and classification? And—which is even better—isn't it the case that for him, as for M. Giraudoux, man's freedom resides not so much in the contingency of his becoming as in the exact realization of his essence. Both recognize first beginnings, natural places, the 'all or nothing' principle, and discontinuity. M. Giraudoux has written the novel of Natural History, Aristotle produced its philosophy. However, Aristotle's was the only philosophy that could stand atop the science of his time: he wanted to systematize the wealth of material that had been amassed by observation and we know that observation, by its nature, culminates in classification; and classification, by *its* nature, appeals to concepts. We are, by contrast, very much at a loss to understand M.

Giraudoux. For four hundred years, philosophers and scholars have been striving to break down rigid conceptual frameworks; to accord preeminence, in all fields, to free creative judgement; to substitute the evolution of species for their fixity. Today, philosophy is foundering, science is shipping water on all sides and morality is drowning. We are everywhere striving to lend the greatest flexibility to our methods and our judgement. No one believes in any sort of pre-established harmony between man and things any longer. No one now dares hope that nature will be accessible to us in its very essence. But suddenly a novelistic universe appears and seduces us with its indefinable charm and air of novelty. We look closer and discover the world of Aristotle, a world that has been buried for four hundred years.

Where has this ghost come from? How has a contemporary writer been able, in all simplicity, to choose to produce fictional illustrations of the views of a Greek philosopher who died three centuries before our era? I have to confess I cannot understand it. It could doubtless be pointed out that we are all Aristotelian at times. One evening we are walking along the streets of Paris and suddenly things turn still, distinct faces towards us. That evening, of all evenings, is a 'Paris evening' and, out of all the streets that climbs up towards Sacré-Coeur, this little street is a 'Montmartre street'. Time has stopped and we are blessed with a moment of happiness, an eternity of happiness. Which of us has not had such a revelation at least once? I say 'revelation', but I am wrong.

Or, rather, it is a revelation that teaches nothing. What I grasp from the pavements, the roadway, the facades of the buildings is merely the concept of street, a concept that has long been in my possession. I have an impression of knowing without there being any knowledge, an intuition of Necessity without any necessity. This human concept, which the street and the evening reflect back like mirrors, dazzles me and prevents me from seeing the inhuman meaning of things, their humble, tenacious thingly smiles. What matter? The street is there and up it climbs—so purely and magnificently a street. There is nothing more to say about it. These unproductive intuitions are comparable not so much to real contemplation as to what our psychologists call illusions of false recognition. Is this the explanation of M. Giraudoux's sensibility? It would be a bold interpretation and I have no idea if it is right. I imagine, too, that a Marxist would call M. Giraudoux's views an urbane rationalism, and that he would explain the rationalism by the triumphant rise of capitalism at the beginning of this century and the urbanity by the very special position M. Giraudoux occupies within the French bourgeoisie: peasant origins, classical culture, a career in the diplomatic corps. I do not know. Perhaps M. Giraudoux knows. Perhaps this writer, so discreet and well hidden behind his fictions, will one day tell us about himself.

March 1940

*

MAN BOUND HAND AND FOOT:
NOTES ON JULES RENARD'S *JOURNAL*

He created the literature of silence. We know how it has prospered since. We have had the theatre of silence and also those enormous bonfires of words that were the Surrealists' poems: the curtain of words went up in flames; behind this veil of fire we were allowed to glimpse a great mute presence: Spirit. Today Blanchot strives to construct peculiar precision machines (that we might call 'silencers', after the devices that make pistols deliver their bullets without a sound) in which the words are carefully chosen to cancel each other out and which resemble those complicated algebraic operations, the product of which has to equal zero. Exquisite forms of terrorism. But Jules Renard isn't a terrorist. He isn't aiming to conquer an unknown silence beyond words; his aim isn't to *invent* silence. He imagines he possesses silence from the outset. It is in him, it is *him*. It is a thing. All that is needed is to pin it down on paper, to copy it with words. This is a realism of silence.

He has generations of mutism behind him. His mother spoke in short peasant sentences, full but few and far between. His father was one of those village eccentrics, as was my paternal grandfather, who, having been disappointed by his marriage contract, never spoke three words to my grandmother in forty-five years— she called him 'my lodger'. He spent his childhood among peasants who, each in their different ways, proclaimed the uselessness of speech. 'When he gets home,' he writes, 'the peasant moves no more than the three-toed sloth or the tardigrade. He loves the darkness, not only out of thrift, but as a preference. His burning eyes can rest.'[1] Take the portrait of old Bulot. A new servant comes to the house:

> 'The first day, she asked, "What am I going to cook you for your tea, then?"
>
> "Potato soup."
>
> The next day she asked, "What am I going to cook you?"
>
> "I told you: potato soup."

1 Jules Renard, *Journal* (16 January 1889). There is a version of this passage in *The Journal of Jules Renard* (Louise Bogan and Elizabeth Roget eds) (Portland: Tin House Books, 2008), p. 25. Since translations into English of this work are only partial and there are various French editions, many of them consisting only of extracts, all references to Renard's *Journal* are made to the date of the entry, so far as I have been able to track it down. [Trans.]

So she got the message and from that point on, every day, off her own bat, she made him his potato soup.'

There was something gnarled and solitary that made him like old Bulot: a real villager's misanthropy. As a country doctor or magistrate or village mayor, he would have adapted perfectly to his functions; perhaps he would have been happy. But this taciturn individual had a taste for writing; he came to Paris to *play* the eccentric, he sought out company to show his loneliness in it; his demanding silence was feared in the circles he frequented; he came to Paris to be silent in writing.

He wanted to shine by works which, amid the loquacious books of the time, were like he was among the salon gossips. Today, such a desire would have led him to seek out a formula for the self-destruction of language. That idea wasn't around in his age.

He thought that brevity in speech came closest to silence and that the most silent sentence was the one that achieved the greatest economy. He believed all his life that style was the art of being brief. And it is no doubt true that the most concise expression is usually the best, though, we must add: concise relative to the idea one is expressing. Thus, a number of the long sentences of Descartes or Proust are extremely short, because one couldn't express in fewer words what they are saying. But Renard wasn't content with this relative conciseness, which tests the sentence against its meaning. He wanted absolute concision: before he had the idea, he set the number of words that were to express it. The only problem to concern him was the one Janet calls the problem of the basket, which he formulates in the following terms: 'How to carry the most bricks in a single basket?' Renard claims he lost all taste for poetry because, he says, 'a line of poetry is still too long.' In novels, what interests him are 'sylistic curiosities'. And it is there they are to be found least, for, in a novel, style remains in the background. But Renard didn't like novels.

Renard's sentence is round and full, with the minimum of internal organization; it resembles those solid, rudimentary animals that have a single hole which serves them as mouth and meatus. There are none of those subordinate clauses that are like dorsal spines or arteries or, sometimes, nerve ganglions. Everything that isn't part of the main proposition seems suspicious in his eyes: it is chatter, useless restrictions, otiose adjunctions, reservations. His beef is really with syntax itself; to this peasant it resembles the refinement of an idler. It was the earthy, people's sentence, the single-cell sentence of old Bulot, he made his own. Words alone are assigned the mission of rendering the nuances and complexity of the idea. Rich words in a poor sentence. This was necessarily his goal: the word is closer to silence than the sentence. The ideal would be for the word itself to be a sentence. In that way, discourse and silence would be united in it, as time and eternity are united in the Kierkegaardian moment. But since we cannot have the word-sentence, let us put into the sentence the fewest, most meaningful words. Let them not restrict themselves to expressing the idea in its nakedness, but let them, by the play of their different meanings—etymological, demotic and scholarly—give us a glimpse of a harmonic 'beyond' of the idea.

What a fine role Malherbe could play at this time:

'Of a word put in its place [he could teach] the power'[2]

And throw into the rubbish bin all the other words that are limp as jellyfish.[3]

The sentence is, then, a super-saturated silence. It never refers on to another: why say in two sentences what could be expressed in one? We are getting to the essential point here: the person who writes by paragraphs or books is, when he traces out a sentence on paper, referred by that sentence to the whole of language. He doesn't dominate language, he is *making* it; these words I write imply all those that came before them and all those I will write afterwards and, moving from one to the next, they imply all words; I need the whole language to understand what is merely an incomplete moment of the language. In this case, silence exists now only as a word within language and *I* situate myself in language,

---

2 This is one of the most famous lines of Boileau's work *Art Poétique*, celebrating the coming of Malherbe (1555–1628) in French literature. [Trans.]

3 Renard, *Journal* (9 August 1893).

in this to-ing and fro-ing of meanings, none of which is complete and each of which requires all the others. But if, like Renard, I think in brusque sentences that hem the total idea between two boundary markers, each sentence, referring to no other, is itself the *whole* language. And I who read it, who write it, condense it with a viewpoint; before it and after it there is emptiness; I decipher it and understand it *from the standpoint of* silence. And the sentence itself, hanging in silence, becomes silence, in the same way as knowledge, when contemplated by Blanchot or Bataille, from the standpoint of non-knowledge— that is to say, of a 'beyond' of knowledge—becomes non-knowledge. For language isn't this loose-limbed sound that sputters for a moment at the height of silence, but a total undertaking on the part of humanity.

It happens, however, that Renard reverses the order of expression in a curious way: his initial aim being silence, it is *in order to remain silent* that he seeks out the right sentence, a momentary drop of silence, and it is *for the sentence* that he seeks out the right idea: 'How empty an idea is: if I didn't have the sentence, I'd go to bed.'[4]

This is because he believes naively that the idea is contained in *one* sentence that expresses it. The sentence, between the two full stops that are its outer limits, seems to him the natural body of the idea. It has never occurred to him that an idea may be embodied in a chapter or a volume, and that it may too—in the sense in which

---

4 Renard, *Journal* (1 December 1891).

Brunschvicg speaks of the 'critical idea'—be inexpressible and simply represent a method of approach to certain problems or, in other words, a rule of discourse.

The idea, for Renard, is an assertive formula in which a certain number of experiences is condensed; similarly, the sentence—which, in so many other writers, is a joint, a passage, a slide, a twist, a hub, a bridge or a rampart within that microcosm that is the paragraph— is merely for him the condensation of certain quantities of ideas. Idea and sentence, body and soul present themselves to him in the form of a maxim or paradox. For example: 'I would so enjoy being good.' This is because he has no ideas. His deliberate, studied, artistic silence masks a natural, helpless silence: he has nothing to say. He thinks in order the better to be silent; this means that 'he speaks to say nothing.'

For, in the end, this preference for dumbness brings him back to chattering. You can chatter in five words just as you can in a hundred lines. You merely have to prefer sentences to ideas. For then the reader encounters the sentence and the idea remains hidden. Renard's *Journal* is a laconic chatter; his entire opus a pointillisme—and there is a rhetoric of this pointillisme, just as there is of the great, thought-out sentence of Louis Guez de Balzac.[5]

---

5 Jean-Louis Guez de Balzac (1597–1654): widely credited with having introduced a major reform of French prose style, particularly through his *Lettres*. [Trans.]

The reader will perhaps be surprised to hear that Renard had nothing to say. It will be asked why certain ages and certain human beings have no message to deliver, when one has only to depict oneself to be original. But perhaps the question is poorly framed. Hearing it, we might have the impression that human nature is fixed, together with the inner eye observing it, and that eye merely has to adapt itself to our darkness to distinguish some new truths. In fact, the eye prefigures and sorts what it sees; and that eye isn't given from the outset. Its way of seeing has to be invented; it is thus one determines *a priori* and by free choice what one sees. The empty ages are the ones that choose to look at themselves with already invented eyes. They can do nothing but refine others' discoveries, for those who provide the eyes at the same time provide the things seen. Throughout the second half of the French nineteenth century, we saw ourselves with the eyes of the London empiricists, with the eyes of John Stuart Mill and the spectacles of Spencer. The writer has only one method: observation; and only one instrument: analysis. One could already detect a certain unease by the time Flaubert and the Goncourt brothers had had their day. In his journal of 27 August 1870, Goncourt notes:

> Zola comes to lunch with me. He talks to me about a series of novels he wants to write, an epic in ten volumes, the natural and social history of a family . . . He tells me: after the analysis of infinitely fine matters of sentiment, as attempted

by Flaubert in *Madame Bovary*; after the analysis of artistic, plastic, sinewy things, as done by yourself; after these *jewel-works*, these finely chiselled volumes, there is no place now for the young. There is nothing more to be done. No constituting or constructing of characters or figures. It is only by quantity of volumes, by creative power that one can speak to the public.

This meeting must have been quite richly comic. But let us take it, in the end, for what it is. It proves to us that, already in 1870, a young writer felt himself obliged to become a wholesaler because there was too much competition in the retail trade. Well and good. But *what then*? After the 10-volume epics? What remained to be done? It is at this moment that Renard appears. He is in the latter ranks of that great literary movement that runs from Flaubert to Maupassant via Zola and the Goncourt brothers. All the exits are closed, all the paths blocked. He enters on his career with a desperate sense that everything has been said and that he has arrived too late. He is obsessed with a desire to be original and by the fear that he cannot possibly manage it. For want of having chosen a new way of seeing, he looks everywhere in vain for new sights. For us, finding as we do that all paths are open to us, believing that everything is still to be said and dizzied at times by these empty spaces stretching out before us, nothing is more alien than the complaints of these men bound hand and foot, restricted to a piece of overworked ground and anxiously on the lookout for a patch of virgin earth. Yet this is Renard's situation: he is scornful of Zola and his obsession with documentary evidence, but he acknowledges nonetheless that the writer must seek out *the truth.* Now, that truth is precisely the exact description of the physical and psychological appearance, as it presents itself to a supposedly impartial observer. So, for Renard, as for the naturalists, reality is appearance, as organized, filtered and sorted by positivist science, and this famous 'realism' to which he adheres is a pure and simple rendering of the phenomenon as such. But in that case, what is there to write about? The analysis of the major psychological or social types no longer needs doing: what new things are there to say about *the* financier, *the* miner, *the* kept woman? Zola has already ploughed that furrow. The study of general sentiments has been exhausted. There remains the detail, the individual, the things that Renard's elders neglected, for the very reason that they had higher ambitions. On 17 January 1889, Renard writes: 'Put at the beginning of the book: I did not see types, but individuals. The scientist generalizes, the artist individualizes.'

This formula may seem to offer something like a forestaste of the famous pages in which Gide calls for monographs.[6] But I believe we should see it rather as a

---

6 André Gide tended to refer to his early works, such as *The Immoralist* or *Strait Is the Gate*, as 'monographs', by contrast with his later novels, such as *The Counterfeiters*, in which multiple points of view are adopted. [Trans.]

confession of impotence. Gide is attracted by what he sees that is positive in the study of the individual. But for Renard and his contemporaries, the individual is what has been left to them by their elders. The proof of this is the uncertainty they are in regarding the nature of these singular realities. Admittedly, in 1889 Renard is cross with Dubus[7] because he 'has theories about woman. Still? Are we not finished with having theories about woman?' But this doesn't prevent him, in 1894, advising his son as follows: 'Fantec, as an author, study just one woman, but go deeply into her and you will know woman.'[8]

So the old dream of arriving at the typical hasn't disappeared. Except that a roundabout route will be adopted: if you scratch long enough at the individual, it crumbles and fades and, beneath the peeling varnish, the universal appears.

On the other hand, Renard seems at other moments to despair of ever being able to generalize his observations. But this is because he came, almost unwittingly, under the influence of a pluralistic, anti-finalistic, pessimistic conception of truth that emerged, at around the same time, out of the collapse of positivism and the difficulties the sciences were beginning to encounter, after a triumphal beginning, in certain fields. He writes, for example, 'Our elders saw the character, the continuous type . . . We see the discontinuous type, with its periods

7 Édouard Dubus (1863–95): a French symbolist poet. [Trans.]
8 Fantec was the pet name of Renard's son Pierre-François. [Trans.]

of calm and its crises, its moments of goodness and of wickedness.'[9]

Truth disappeared with Science. Sciences and truths remain. We must admit that this pluralism is still very fragile in Renard, since at the same time he accepts determinism. True pluralism can only be based on a partial indeterminacy of the universe and on human freedom. But Renard didn't go so far into this. And neither did Anatole France, who in *La Vie littéraire* in 1891 (the passage from Renard quoted above is from 1892) wrote:

> It has been said that there are brains that are impermeably partitioned. The subtlest fluid that fills one of the compartments does not soak through to the others at all. And when, in the presence of M. Théodule Ribot, an ardent rationalist expressed astonishment that brains of this kind existed, the master of experimental philosophy replied, with a gentle smile: 'Nothing is less surprising. Is it not, rather, a highly spiritualistic conception that wishes to establish unity in a human intelligence? Why will you not allow a man to be double, triple or quadruple?[10]

This is a page we may treasure for its stupidity, since it shows us that experimental pluralism was directed expressly against spiritualist rationalism. This whole

---

9 Renard, *Journal* (29 February 1892).

10 Anatole France, 'Blaise Pascal et M. Joseph Bertrand', in *La Vie littéraire. Quatrième série* (Paris: Calmann-Lévy, 1892).

pessimistic current of thinking was to lead to Metchnikoff's *Disharmonies in the Nature of Man*.[11] And it was
indeed a study of the 'disharmonies in nature' that
Renard wanted to undertake. In this way he will provide
a theoretical justification for his exclusive taste for snap-
shots: 'In pieces,' he exclaims, 'in little pieces, tiny pieces.'

This brings us back by another route, to which he
refers pretentiously as his nihilism, to our starting point:
pointillisme and the sentence conceived as a work of art
sufficient unto itself. If human nature is, first and foremost, disorder and disharmony, it is consequently no
longer possible to write novels. Renard never tires of
repeating that the novel has had its day, since it requires
a continuous development. If man is merely a chopped-
up series of moments, it would be better to produce
short stories: 'Produce a volume with shorter and shorter
tales and entitle it *The Rolling Mill*.'

In the end we shall be back to the simple sentence.
Renard, they said, would end up writing, 'The hen lays.'
And so the circle is closed: in this instantaneous universe,
where nothing is true and nothing is real but the instant,
the only form of art possible is *notation*. The sentence,
which can be read in an instant and is separated from
other sentences by a twofold void, has as its content the
instantaneous impression that I catch 'on the fly'. Hence,

---

11 The essay mentioned was published in English as Part One of Élie
Metchnikoff (Ilya Mechnikov), *The Nature of Man: Studies in Opti-
mistic Philosophy* (New York: Putnam, 1910), pp. 1–136. [Trans.]

the whole of Renard's psychology will be made up of notations. He examines himself, analyses himself, catches himself out—but always on the fly. Which is just too bad: he notes down his momentary jealousies, his puerile or petty desires, the jokes he makes to amuse the maid; with little effort, he acquires a reputation for fierceness. But why should we be surprised: this is what he chose to see, what he chose to be in his own eyes. And that choice was dictated by aesthetic considerations, not by a moral resolve. For, in the end, he was also a constant and more or less faithful husband, a good father and a zealous writer. In other words, he existed on the level Kierkegaard refers to as the level 'of repetition' and Heidegger the level 'of project' . . . These vague outbursts of egotism count so very little for the person whose life is an enterprise. And, in a sense, everyone's life is an enterprise. 'Swinish' psychology is merely a littérateur's invention. By being resolutely blind to the *composed* aspect of his existence, the continuity of his designs, Renard failed to grasp himself accurately and has left us an unfair picture of himself: our moods have importance only if we pay special heed to them. And we should not consider him or judge him by his moods, but as a man who chose to pay attention to his moods.

Besides, the study of the passions and the stirrings of the soul never concerned him much. From his peasant childhood he had retained a liking for animals and for country things; he likes to speak of them, to describe them. But, here again, he was too late. The writers of the preceding generation—Flaubert, Zola and Dickens—had undertaken an enormous inventory of the real: it was a matter of conquering new regions for art and rendering literary language sufficiently supple to describe such lowly objects as a machine, a garden or a kitchen. In this regard, Flaubert's *Sentimental Education* figured as a manifesto. Everything had come into the novel: it had made the public house its own with *L'Assommoir*, the mines with *Germinal* and the great department stores with *Au Bonheur des Dames*.[12] It was a picture painted with broad brush strokes; more than this, it was a classification. The only task left for Renard's contemporaries was one of refining. It could have been the starting point for a form of new art. And indeed, by contrast with his predecessors, who had been concerned above all to put everything in its place, to count out the kitchen utensils, to enumerate the flowers in the garden, and who experienced a simple delight in naming tools by their technical names, Renard, when faced with the individual object, feels the need to grasp it deeply, to get inside the stuff of it. He is no longer concerned with counting the glasses on the bar and the various drinks that are served in the bar; he no longer considers each object in its relation to others within a detailed inventory; and he knows nothing, either, of the descriptions of 'atmosphere' that Barrès will make fashionable some years later: to him the glass he is looking at seems severed from its ties to the

12 These are all novels by Zola, dating from 1877, 1885 and 1883, respectively. [Trans.]

rest of the world. It is a thing alone and closed in on itself like a sentence. And Renard's sole ambition is that his sentence shall convey more closely, precisely and profoundly the inner nature of the glass. In the very first pages of his *Journal* we see him bent upon sharpening the instrument that will cut into the material, a thing that shows up in these brief notes: 'the strong smell of dry faggots' or 'the quivering of the water beneath the ice'. One can only sympathize with these clumsy efforts to make things bleed. They are at the origin of many more modern endeavours. But Renard is hampered by his very realism: to arrive at this visionary communion with things, one would have to free oneself from Tainean metaphysics.[13] The object would have to have a heart of darkness; it would have to be something other than a pure sensory appearance, a collection of sensations. The profundity Renard senses and seeks in the tiniest pebble, in a spider or a dragonfly, is denied to these things by his timid, positive philosophy. You have to invent the heart of things if you want to discover it one day. Audiberti[14] tells us something about milk when he speaks of its 'secret blackness'. But, for Renard, milk is hopelessly white, since it is merely what it seems. Hence the essential character of his images. Admittedly, they are, first

---

13 The reference is to the great French historian Hippolyte Taine (1828–93). [Trans.]

14 The reference is to the poem 'Du côté de Lariboisière' by Jacques Audiberti (1899–1965), in the collection *Race des Hommes* (Paris: Gallimard, 1937). [Trans.]

and foremost, a way of abbreviating. When he writes, 'This man of genius is an eagle stupid as a goose', we see immediately the brevity these words eagle and goose achieve. The image is, for Renard, among other things, a foreshortening of thinking. And, as a result, this scholarly style, this 'calligraphy' as Arène[15] calls it, is akin to the mythical, proverbial speech of the peasant; each of his sentences is a little fable. But this isn't the main thing. In Renard's writing, the image is a timid attempt at reconstruction. And the reconstruction always miscarries. The aim is, in fact, to penetrate the real. But in terms of Tainean metaphysics, the real is, primarily, something that is observed. That was the wisdom of the age, a literary version of empiricism. And the poor man observes as much as he can: it is on the 17th of *January* that he speaks of the quivering of the water beneath the ice, on the 13th of *May* that he speaks of lilies of the valley. He wouldn't take it into his head to speak of flowers in winter or of ice in midsummer. Yet, everyone today knows that you cannot penetrate reality by passive observation of it: the best of poets is either distracted or fascinated; at any rate, he isn't an observer. Moreover, it matters little that Renard is nihilistic and pessimistic: he believes obediently in the world of science; he is even convinced that the scientific world and the world he observes are one and the same. The sounds striking his ear are, he knows, vibrations of the air; the colours that

15 Paul-August Arène (1843–96): a poet and critic who wrote in both French and Provençal. [Trans.]

meet his eyes are vibrations of the ether. And so he will find *nothing*: his universe is suffocating in the philosophical and scientific brace he has imposed on it. Observation yields it up to him in its commonplace outlines; the universe he *sees* is everyone's universe. And for what he doesn't see he trusts to science. In a word, the real he confronts is entirely constructed already by common sense *chosisme*. And so most of his notations are made up of two parts of a sentence, the first of which—solid, precise and definite—conveys the object as it appears to common sense, and the second of which, joined to the other by the words 'like' or 'as', is the image properly so-called. But precisely because all the information is assembled in the first part of the sentence, the second teaches us nothing; precisely because the object is pre-constituted, the image cannot reveal its structures to us. Take the following, for example: 'A spider slides along an invisible thread, as though it were swimming in the air.'

The animal is first named; its movement is described in precise terms and, beyond mere appearances, there is even a supposition about what we cannot see, for previous experience, together with specialist studies, teaches us that spiders move about on the end of a thread. Nothing could be more positive or reassuring than this first part of the sentence. The second part, with the word 'swimming', serves, conversely, to make the strange resistance the air seems to mount against the spider very different from the resistance it mounts, for example, against the bird or the fly. Only this part is cancelled out by the previous part. Since we are *informed* that the spider is sliding on the end of a thread, since the existence of that invisible thread is revealed to us, and since we are given to understand that this is the reality and the truth, then the image remains up in the air and has no solid basis. Even before we meet it, it is exposed as a mythic translation of a mere *semblance*, if not, indeed, as something wholly unreal—in a word, a fantasy of the author. In this way, the sentence is divided into strong and weak sections, since the first term stands solidly in a social and scientific universe the author takes seriously, while the second goes up in pleasant smoke. This is the warping that threatens all Renard's images and deflects them towards the comical; the 'graciousness' that makes them so many escapes from a tedious, perfectly known reality into an entirely imaginary world that can throw no light whatever on alleged reality.

In 1892, he writes: 'Replace the existing laws with non-existent ones.' And this is what he does in each of his similes, since he puts the real law, the scientific explanation, on the one side and the law he invents on the other. He will note that, 'to faint is to drown in the open air.' He will describe as 'delightful' Saint-Pol Roux's expression, 'The trees exchange birds, as they might exchange words.' He will eventually write: 'The bushes seemed drunken with sun, tossed about as though indisposed and spewed hawthorn, a white foam', which is positively horrendous and *means nothing* because the image develops under its own impetus. Note the 'seemed', aimed at reassuring the reader and Renard himself by warning them from the outset that they will remain in the realm of pure fantasy and that bushes don't spew anything. Note, too, the clumsy juxtaposition of real and imaginary: 'hawthorn, a white foam'. Though Renard compares this flowery froth to foam, he does so after first having named it and attached it to a family, a genus and a kingdom. And, by so doing, he cancels his image, renders it unreal. This is what he thought of as poetry: it was precisely the opposite; there is poetry only when one denies preeminence to the scientific interpretation of reality and treats all systems of inter-pretation as absolutely equivalent. And yet, at the source of this horrendous image we can sense something like an immediate apprehension of a certain nature. There is, in fact, something nauseating in the *existence* in full sunshine of bushes that are dusty and sticky with sap. These tepid plants are already herbal infusions, and yet all the white dusts of the summer coagulate on them. This is something a Francis Ponge would, in our day, convey admirably. By contrast, Renard's attempt miscar-ries before he has even realized what he was wanting to do, because it is tainted at its heart. What it needed was for Renard to lose himself, for him to confront the object alone. But Renard never loses himself. Just watch him running after the red ribbon[16] and weeping with emotion

16 A reference to the red ribbon of the Légion d'honneur, the highest decoration available to French citizens and awarded for excellent con-duct in either the civil or military spheres. [Trans.]

when he is finally awarded it: he may well be able to escape momentarily into the imagination, but he is a man who needs the protection of science and the whole social apparatus. If, like Rimbaud, he had rejected escape, if he had taken issue directly with alleged 'reality', if he had exploded its bourgeois, scientistic frames, he would perhaps have achieved the Proustian 'immediate' or the surrealism of the *Paysan de Paris*;[17] he would perhaps have divined that 'substance' behind things that Rilke or Hofmannsthal[18] were seeking. But he didn't even know what he was looking for; and if he is at the origin of modern literature, he is so because he had a vague presentiment of a field to which he forbade himself access.

The fact is also that Renard never lived alone. He was a member of an 'elite'; he regarded himself as an *artist*. This artist notion came from the Goncourt brothers. It bears their stamp of pretentious, vulgar stupidity. It is all that remains of the *poète maudit* of the heroic age: the Art for Art's sake movement took that course. What weighs on the heads of Renard and his friends is merely

17 *Le Paysan de Paris* is a work by Louis Aragon, serialized initially in the *Revue Européenne* (1924–25) and published in book form in 1926. [Trans.]

18 Rainer Maria Rilke (1875– 1926): born in Prague, he was one of the greatest German-language poets of the twentieth century; Hugo von Hofmannsthal (1874–1929): another of the great writers of the Austro-Hungarian empire, he was a prolific novelist, poet, librettist and essayist. [Trans.]

a comfortable, *embourgeoisé*, white-magic curse: no longer that of the solitary wizard, but a mark of election. You are cursed if you have a particularly friable 'brain' and refined nerves. And, in fact, this '*artist*' idea isn't just the debased relic of a great religious myth—that of the poet, the *vates*.[19] It is, above all, the prism through which a small group of prosperous, cultivated bourgeois—who write—conceive and recognize themselves as the elite of the Third Republic. It may surprise us today: Jules Romains or André Malraux would probably agree that they are artists, since it is, after all, generally accepted that there is an *art* of writing. But it doesn't seem that they view themselves from this standpoint. A more thoroughgoing division of labour has come about in our day—particularly since the 1914–18 war. The contemporary writer is concerned, above all, to present his readers with a complete image of the human condition. In so doing, he 'commits himself'. Today a book that doesn't involve a commitment is something we rather scorn. As for beauty, it comes as something additional, when that is possible. It is the beauty and the pleasure of art that Jules Renard puts at the forefront of his concerns. The writer of 1895 is neither a prophet, nor a damned soul, nor a fighter: he is an initiate. He stands apart from the masses less by what he does than by the pleasure he takes in doing it. It is this aesthetic delight, the product of his 'exquisite', highly-strung

---

19 *Vates*: implied is the poet as prophet, seer or soothsayer. [Trans.]

nerves, that makes him an exceptional creature. And Renard is angered by the thought that an old violinist can claim to feel a more intense artistic pleasure than his own circle:

> Comparison between music and literature. These people would have us believe that their emotions are more complete than ours . . . I find it hard to believe that this little man, who is barely alive, experiences greater delight in art than Victor Hugo or Lamartine, who didn't like music.

So here is Renard bound hand and foot: the fact is that, despite a number of feeble denials, he is a realist. Now, the essence of the realist is that he doesn't act. He contemplates, since he wishes to portray reality as it is or, in other words, as it appears to an impartial witness. He has—this is his duty as a literary man—to *neutralize* himself. He is not, he must never be 'a part of the action'. He floats above the parties, above classes, and by that very fact asserts himself as bourgeois, since the specific characteristic of the bourgeois is to deny the existence of the bourgeois class. His contemplation is of a particular kind: it is an intuitive delight accompanied by aesthetic emotion. Only, since the realist is pessimistic, he sees only disorder and ugliness in the world. His mission, then, is to transpose real objects—just as they are—into sentences of a form capable of giving him aesthetic pleasure. The realist finds his pleasure in *writing*, not in looking, and what enables him to appreciate the value of the sentence he writes is the delight that sentence affords him. In this way, this nihilistic realism leads Renard, like Flaubert before him, to an entirely formal conception of beauty. The material is grim and nasty, but these elite sensibilities thrill to the phrase that can deck it out magnificently. The aim is to dress up reality. Flaubert's fine oratorical period becomes, then, Renard's little instantaneous silence. But that silence, too, aspires to be a thing of marble. And so we are back, once more, at our starting point: a fine sentence, for Renard, is the one that can be carved on a stone. Beauty is economy of thought; it is a tiny silence, carved in stone or bronze, suspended amid the great silence of Nature.

He fell silent, he did nothing. His project was to destroy himself. Trussed up and gagged by his family, his age and his milieu, his bias towards psychological analysis and his marriage, sterilized by his *Journal*, he found resources only in dreams. His images that were at first to sink themselves like claws into the real, quickly became instant daydreams, at the margin of things. But he was too afraid of getting out of his depth to think of constructing a universe beyond the world that was personal to him. He very soon came back to objects, his friends, his decoration, and his most persistent dreams—because they were the least dangerous—confined themselves to toying with the idea of a pleasant little dull adultery that he seldom had the courage to commit. Similarly, his *Journal*, which had seemed set to become an exercise in clear-sighted severity, very quickly became a lukewarm, shady corner of shame-faced complicity with himself. This is the other side to the fearful family silences of Monsieur Lepic.[20] In it he lays himself bare, though that isn't immediately evident, since the style is formally dressed. He heaps abuse on his life; realism, in its death throes, chose him to die through. And yet— whether through this determined attempt to destroy himself, this systematic fragmentation of the great Flaubertian period, or his ever-deceived presentiment of individual concreteness beyond the abstract appearances of empiricism—this moribund character attests to a kind of catastrophe that afflicted the *fin-de-siècle* writers and is, directly or indirectly, at the origin of contemporary literature.

1945

---

20 The central character of Renard's most famous work, *Poil de Carotte*. [Trans.]

✳

A NOTE ON SOURCES

'Monsieur François Mauriac and Freedom'

Originally published as 'M. François Mauriac et la liberté' in *Situations I* (Paris: Gallimard, 1947), pp. 33–52.

First published in English translation in *Critical Essays* (London: Seagull Books, 2010), pp. 47–84.

'Gide Alive'

Originally published as 'Gide vivant' in *Situations IV* (Paris: Gallimard, 1964), pp. 85–9.

First published in English translation in *Portraits* (London: Seagull Books, 2009), pp. 115–22.

'Portrait of a Man Unknown'

Originally published as 'Portrait d'un inconnu' in *Situations IV* (Paris: Gallimard, 1964), pp. 9–16.

First published in English translation in *Portraits* (London: Seagull Books, 2009), pp. 3–14.

'Monsieur Jean Giraudoux and the Philosophy of Aristotle: On *Choix des Élues*'

Originally published as 'Monsieur Jean Giraudoux et la philosophie d'Aristotle' in *Situations I* (Paris: Gallimard, 1947), pp. 76–91.

First published in English translation in *Critical Essays* (London: Seagull Books, 2010), pp. 122–47.

'Man Bound Hand and Foot:
Notes on Jules Renard's *Journal*'

Originally published as 'L'homme ligoté. Notes sur le *Journal* de Jules Renard' in *Situations I* (Paris: Gallimard, 1947), pp. 271–88.

First published in English translation in *Critical Essays* (London: Seagull Books, 2010), pp. 466–97.